THE 10 BEST
WAYS TO DEFEAT
MULTIPLE ATTACKERS

SAMMY FRANCO

Also by Sammy Franco

Cane Fighting
Double End Bag Training
The Heavy Bag Bible
The Widow Maker Compendium
Invincible: Mental Toughness Techniques for Peak Performance
Unleash Hell: A Step-by-Step Guide to Devastating Widow Maker Combinations
Feral Fighting: Advanced Widow Maker Fighting Techniques
The Widow Maker Program: Extreme Self-Defense for Deadly Force Situations
Savage Street Fighting: Tactical Savagery as a Last Resort
Heavy Bag Workout
Heavy Bag Combinations
Heavy Bag Training
The Complete Body Opponent Bag Book
Stand and Deliver: A Street Warrior's Guide to Tactical Combat Stances
Maximum Damage: Hidden Secrets Behind Brutal Fighting Combinations
First Strike: End a Fight in Ten Seconds or Less!
The Bigger They Are, The Harder They Fall
Self-Defense Tips and Tricks
Kubotan Power: Quick & Simple Steps to Mastering the Kubotan Keychain
Gun Safety: For Home Defense and Concealed Carry
Out of the Cage: A Guide to Beating a Mixed Martial Artist on the Street
Warrior Wisdom: Inspiring Ideas from the World's Greatest Warriors
War Machine: How to Transform Yourself Into a Vicious and Deadly Street Fighter
1001 Street Fighting Secrets
When Seconds Count: Self-Defense for the Real World
Killer Instinct: Unarmed Combat for Street Survival
Street Lethal: Unarmed Urban Combat

The 10 Best Ways To Defeat Multiple Attackers (10 Best Series #2)
Copyright © 2017 by Sammy Franco
ISBN: 978-1-941845-48-6
Printed in the United States of America

Published by Contemporary Fighting Arts, LLC.
Visit us Online at: **SammyFranco.com**

For author interviews or publicity information, please send inquiries in care of the publisher.

Contents

"Let your plans be dark and impenetrable as night, and when you move, fall like a thunderbolt."

– Sun Tzu, The Art of War

Warning!

The self-defense techniques, tactics, methods, and information described and depicted in this book can be dangerous and could result in serious injury and or death and should not be used or practiced in any way without the guidance of a professional reality based self-defense instructor.

The author, publisher, and distributors of this book disclaim any liability from loss, injury, or damage, personal or otherwise, resulting from the information and procedures in this book. *This book is for academic study only.*

Before you begin any exercise program, including those suggested in this book, it is important to check with your physician to see if you have any condition that might be aggravated by strenuous exercise.

Why You Need This Book

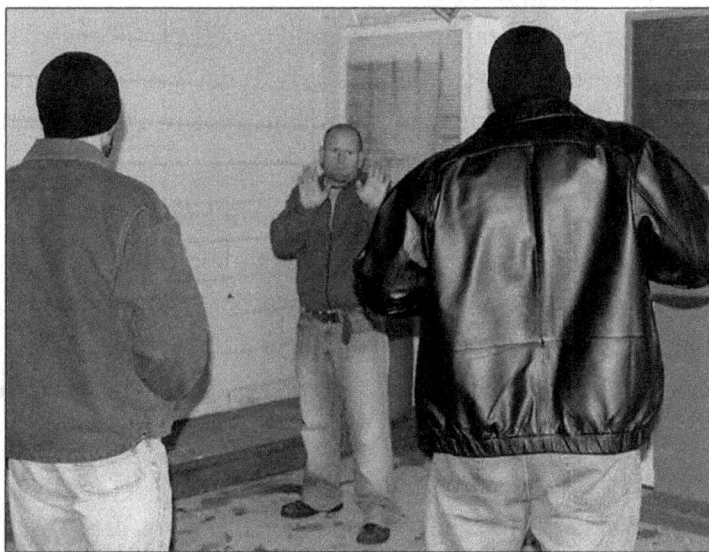

The 10 Best Ways To Defeat Multiple Attackers is the second book in my 10 Best Book Series. This unique book offers you the most practical and effective methods for fighting multiple attackers.

This book isn't about sport fighting, flashy martial arts moves or traditional fighting rituals. Instead, it arms you with simple techniques and effective strategies to protect you and your loved from the immediate threat of unlawful deadly criminal attack. Best of all, you do not have to be a martial arts or self-defense expert to master these life-saving principles.

Some of you might think you are already prepared to handle a multiple attacker situation. After all, you're in great shape and have practiced the martial arts for years. But, unless you have mastered the specific principles and strategies featured in this book, you are not as prepared as you should be. The 10 Best Ways To

Defeat Multiple Attackers teaches you exactly what you need to know, so you'll be prepared if and when that fateful days arrives.

The information and techniques featured in this book are based on my 30+ years of research, training and teaching reality based self-defense. I have taught these unique survival concepts to thousands of my students, and I'm confident they will help you in a desperate time of need.

Regardless of your training background or level of experience. The techniques and strategies featured in this book are practical and straightforward and can be seamlessly incorporated into your current martial arts, self-defense or survival program. In fact, integrating these principles and their related concepts will significantly improve your odds of prevailing in any high risk self-defense situation.

Again, the information presented in this book is not intended for sports combat, tournament competitions, or any self-defense situation that does not justifiably warrant the use of deadly force.

Deadly force is defined as violent action known to create a substantial risk of causing death or serious bodily harm. A person may use deadly force in self-defense only if retaliating against another's deadly force.

Much of the information contained in this book is lethal and should only be used to protect yourself or a loved one from immediate risk of unlawful deadly criminal attack. Remember, the decision to use deadly force must always be a last resort; after all other means of avoiding violence has been thoroughly exhausted.

Be Safe!

Sammy Franco

Introduction
Contemporary Fighting Arts

The 10 Best Ways to Defeat Multiple Attackers

Exploring Contemporary Fighting Arts

Before diving head first into this book, I'd like to first introduce you to my unique system of fighting, Contemporary Fighting Arts (CFA). I hope it will give you a greater understanding and appreciation of the material covered in this book. And for those of you who are already familiar with CFA, you can skip to the next chapter.

Contemporary Fighting Arts® (CFA), is a state-of-the-art combat system that was introduced to the world in 1983. This sophisticated and practical system of self-defense is designed specifically to provide efficient and effective methods to avoid, defuse, confront, and neutralize both armed and unarmed assailants in a variety of deadly situations and circumstances.

Unlike karate, kung-fu, mixed martial arts and the like, CFA is the first offensive-based American martial art that is specifically designed for the violence that plagues our cruel city streets. CFA dispenses with the extraneous and the impractical and focuses on real-life street fighting.

Every tool, technique and tactic found within the CFA system must meet three essential criteria for fighting: efficiency, effectiveness, and safety. Efficiency means that the techniques permit you to reach your combative objective quickly and economically. Effectiveness means that the elements of the system will produce the desired effect. Finally, Safety means that the combative elements provide the least amount of danger and risk for you - the fighter.

CFA is not about mind-numbing tournaments or senseless competition. It does not require you to waste time and energy practicing forms (katas) or other impractical rituals. There are no

3

theatrical kicks or exotic techniques. Finally, CFA does not adhere blindly to tradition for tradition's sake. Simply put, it is a scientific yet pragmatic approach to staying alive on the streets.

CFA has been taught to people of all walks of life. Some include the U.S. Border Patrol, police officers, deputy sheriffs, security guards, military personnel, private investigators, surgeons, lawyers, college professors, airline pilots, as well as black belts, boxers, and kick boxers. CFA's broad appeal results from its ability to teach people how to really fight.

It's All In The Name!

Before discussing the three components that make up Contemporary Fighting Arts, it is important to understand how CFA acquired its unique name. To begin, the first word, "Contemporary," was selected because it refers to the system's modern, up-to-date orientation. Unlike traditional martial arts, CFA is specifically designed to meet the challenges of our modern world.

The second term, "Fighting," was chosen because it accurately describes the system's combat orientation. After all, why not just call it Contemporary Martial Arts? There are two reasons for this. First, the word "martial" conjures up images of traditional and impractical martial art forms that are antithetical to the system. Second, why dilute a perfectly functional name when the word "fighting" defines the system so succinctly? Contemporary Fighting Arts is about teaching people how to really fight.

Let's look at the last word, "Arts." In the subjective sense, "art" refers to the combat skills that are acquired through arduous study, practice, and observation. The bottom line is that effective street fighting skills will require consistent practice and attention. Take, for example, something as seemingly basic as an elbow strike, which will actually require hundreds of hours of practice to perfect.

The pluralization of the word "Art" reflects CFA's protean instruction. The various components of CFA's training (i.e., firearms training, stick fighting, ground fighting, natural body weapon mastery, and so on) have all truly earned their status as individual art forms and, as such, require years of consistent study and practice to perfect. To acquire a greater understanding of CFA, here is an overview of the system's three vital components: the physical, the mental, and the spiritual.

Police officers need practical and effective defensive tactics for dealing with violent street criminals. This is why many law enforcement officers seek out Contemporary Fighting Arts training.

The Physical Component

The physical component of CFA focuses on the physical development of a fighter, including physical fitness, weapon and

The 10 Best Ways to Defeat Multiple Attackers

technique mastery, and self-defense attributes.

Physical Fitness

If you are going to prevail in a street fight, you must be physically fit. It's that simple. In fact, you will never master the tools and skills of combat unless you're in excellent physical shape. On the average, you will have to spend more than an hour a day to achieve maximum fitness.

In CFA physical fitness comprises the following three broad components: cardiorespiratory conditioning, muscular/skeletal conditioning, and proper body composition.

The cardiorespiratory system includes the heart, lungs, and circulatory system, which undergo tremendous stress during the course of a street fight. So you're going to have to run, jog, bike, swim, or skip rope to develop sound cardiorespiratory conditioning. Each aerobic workout should last a minimum of 30 minutes and be performed at least four times per week.

The second component of physical fitness is muscular/skeletal conditioning. In the streets, the strong survive and the rest go to the morgue. To strengthen your bones and muscles to withstand the rigors of a real fight, your program must include progressive resistance (weight training) and calisthenics. You will also need a stretching program designed to loosen up every muscle group. You can't kick, punch, ground fight, or otherwise execute the necessary body mechanics if you're "tight" or inflexible. Stretching on a regular basis will also increase the muscles' range of motion, improve circulation, reduce the possibility of injury, and relieve daily stress.

The final component of physical fitness is proper body composition: simply, the ratio of fat to lean body tissue. Your diet and training regimen will affect your level or percentage of body fat significantly. A sensible and consistent exercise program

6

accompanied by a healthy and balanced diet will facilitate proper body composition. Do not neglect this important aspect of physical fitness.

Weapon and Technique Mastery

You won't stand a chance against a vicious assailant if you don't master the weapons and tools of fighting. In CFA, we teach our students both armed and unarmed methods of combat. Unarmed fighting requires that you master a complete arsenal of natural body weapons and techniques. In conjunction, you must also learn the various stances, hand positioning, footwork, body mechanics, defensive structure, locks, chokes, and various holds. Keep in mind that something as simple as a basic punch will actually require hundreds of hours to perfect.

Range proficiency is another important aspect of weapon and technique mastery. Briefly, range proficiency is the ability to fight effectively in all three ranges of unarmed fighting. Although punching range tools are emphasized in CFA, kicking and grappling ranges cannot be neglected. Our kicking range tools consist of deceptive and powerful low-line kicks. Grappling range tools include head-butts, elbows, knees, foot stomps, biting, tearing, gouging, and crushing tactics.

Although CFA focuses on striking, we also teach our students a myriad of chokes, locks, and holds that can be used in a ground fight. While such grappling range submission techniques are not the most preferred methods of dealing with a ground fighting situation, they must be studied for the following six reasons: (1) level of force - many ground fighting situations do not justify the use of deadly force. In such instances, you must apply various non-lethal submission holds, (2) nature of the beast - in order to escape any choke, lock or hold, you must first know how to apply them yourself, (3) occupational requirement- some professional occupations (police, security, etc.) require that you possess a working knowledge of various submission techniques, (4) subduing a friend or relative - in many cases it is best to restrain and control a friend or relative with a submission hold instead of striking him with a natural body weapon, (5) anatomical orientation - practicing various chokes, locks and holds will help you develop a strong orientation of the human anatomy, and (6) refutation requirement - finally, if you are going to criticize the combative limitations of any submission hold, you better be sure that you can perform it yourself.

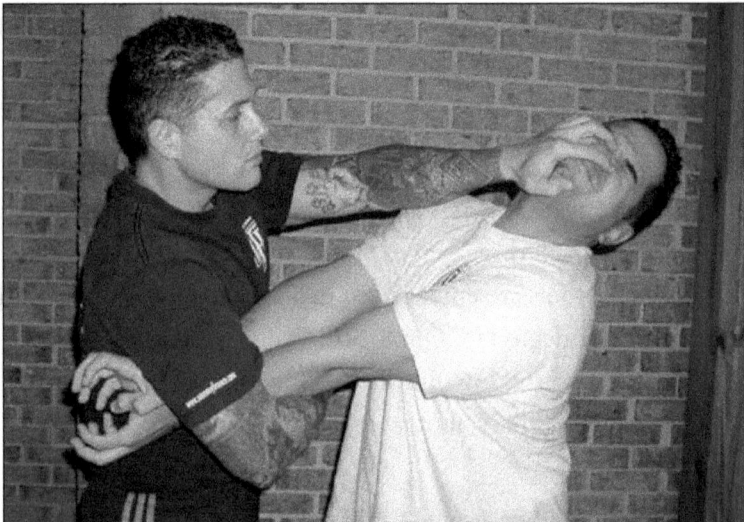

Contemporary Fighting Arts is more than a self defense system, its a one-of-a-kind martial arts style geared for real world self defense.

Defensive tools and skills are also taught. Our defensive structure is efficient, uncomplicated, and impenetrable. It provides the fighter maximum protection while allowing complete freedom of choice for acquiring offensive control. Our defensive structure is based on distance, parrying, blocking, evading, mobility, and stance structure.

Simplicity is always the key.

Students are also instructed in specific methods of armed fighting. For example, CFA provides instruction about firearms for personal and household protection. We provide specific guidelines for handgun purchasing, operation, nomenclature, proper caliber, shooting fundamentals, cleaning, and safe storage. Our firearm program also focuses on owner responsibility and the legal ramifications regarding the use of deadly force.

CFA's weapons program also consists of natural body weapons, knives and edged weapons, single and double stick, makeshift weaponry, the side-handle baton, and oleoresin capsicum (OC) spray.

Combat Attributes

Your offensive and defensive tools are useless unless they are used strategically. For any tool or technique to be effective in a real fight, it must be accompanied by specific attributes. Attributes are qualities that enhance a particular tool, technique, or maneuver. Some examples include speed, power, timing, coordination, accuracy, non-telegraphic movement, balance, and target orientation.

CFA also has a wide variety of training drills and methodologies designed to develop and sharpen these combat attributes. For example, our students learn to ground fight while blindfolded, spar with one arm tied down, and fight while handcuffed.

Reality is the key. For example, in class students participate in full-contact exercises against fully padded assailants, and real weapon disarms are rehearsed and analyzed in a variety of dangerous scenarios. Students also train with a large variety of equipment, including heavy bags, double-end bags, uppercut bags, pummel bags, focus mitts, striking shields, mirrors, rattan sticks, foam and plastic bats, kicking pads, knife drones, trigger-sensitive (mock) guns, boxing and digit gloves, full-body armor, and hundreds of different environmental props.

There are more than two hundred unique training methodologies used in Contemporary Fighting Arts. Each one is scientifically designed to prepare students for the hard-core realities of real world combat. There are also three specific training methodologies used to develop and sharpen the fundamental attributes and skills of armed and unarmed fighting, including proficiency training, conditioning training, and street training.

CFA has a several unique military combat training programs. Our mission is to provide today's modern soldier with the knowledge, skills and attitude necessary to survive a wide variety of real world combat scenarios. Our military program is designed to provide the modern soldier with the safest and most effective skills and tactics to control and decentralize armed and unarmed enemies.

Proficiency training can be used for both armed and unarmed skills. When conducted properly, proficiency training develops speed, power, accuracy, non-telegraphic movement, balance, and general psychomotor skill. The training objective is to sharpen one specific body weapon, maneuver, or technique at a time by executing it over and over for a prescribed number of repetitions. Each time the technique or maneuver is executed with "clean" form at various speeds. Movements are also performed with the eyes closed to develop a kinesthetic "feel" for the action. Proficiency training can be accomplished through the use of various types of equipment, including the heavy bag, double-end bag, focus mitts, training knives, real and mock pistols, striking shields, shin and knee guards, foam and plastic bats, mannequin heads, and so on.

Conditioning training develops endurance, fluidity, rhythm, distancing, timing, speed, footwork, and balance. In most cases, this type of training requires the student to deliver a variety of fighting combinations for three- or four-minute rounds separated by 30-second breaks. Like proficiency training, this type of training can also be performed at various speeds. A good workout consists of at least five rounds. Conditioning training can be performed on the bags with full-contact sparring gear, rubber training knives, focus mitts, kicking shields, and shin guards, or against imaginary assailants in shadow fighting.

Conditioning training is not necessarily limited to just three- or four-minute rounds. For example, CFA's ground fighting training can last as long as 30 minutes. The bottom line is that it all depends on what you are training for.

Street training is the final preparation for the real thing. Since many violent altercations are explosive, lasting an average of 20 seconds, you must prepare for this possible scenario. This means delivering explosive and powerful compound attacks with vicious intent for approximately 20 seconds, resting one minute, and then repeating the process.

Street training prepares you for the stress and immediate fatigue of a real fight. It also develops speed, power, explosiveness, target selection and recognition, timing, footwork, pacing, and breath

The 10 Best Ways to Defeat Multiple Attackers

control. You should practice this methodology in different lighting, on different terrains, and in different environmental settings. You can use different types of training equipment as well. For example, you can prepare yourself for multiple assailants by having your training partners attack you with focus mitts from a variety of angles, ranges, and target postures. For 20 seconds, go after them with vicious low-line kicks, powerful punches, and devastating strikes.

When all is said and done, the physical component creates a fighter who is physically fit and armed with a lethal arsenal of tools, techniques, and weapons that can be deployed with destructive results.

The Mental Component

The mental component of CFA focuses on the cerebral aspects of a fighter, developing killer instinct, strategic/tactical awareness, analysis and integration skills, philosophy, and cognitive skills.

The Killer Instinct

Deep within each of us is a cold and deadly primal power known as the "killer instinct." The killer instinct is a vicious combat mentality that surges to your consciousness and turns you into a fierce fighter who is free of fear, anger, and apprehension. If you want to survive the horrifying dynamics of real criminal violence, you must cultivate and utilize this instinctive killer mentality.

There are 14 characteristics of CFA's killer instinct. They are: (1) clear and lucid thinking, (2) heightened situational awareness, (3) adrenaline surge, (4) mobilized body, (5) psychomotor control, (6) absence of distraction, (7) tunnel vision, (8) fearless mind-set, (9) tactical implementation, (10) the lack of emotion, (11) breath control, (12) pseudospeciation, (13) viciousness, and (14) pain tolerance.

Visualization and crisis rehearsal are just two techniques used to develop, refine, and channel this extraordinary source of strength and energy so that it can be used to its full potential.

Strategic/Tactical Awareness

Strategy is the bedrock of preparedness. In CFA, there are three unique categories of strategic awareness that will diminish the likelihood of criminal victimization. They are criminal awareness, situational awareness, and self-awareness. When developed, these essential skills prepare you to assess a wide variety of threats instantaneously and accurately. Once you've made a proper threat assessment, you will be able to choose one of the following five self-defense options: comply, escape, de-escalate, assert, or fight back.

CFA also teaches students to assess a variety of other important factors, including the assailant's demeanor, intent, range, positioning and weapon capability, as well as such environmental issues as escape routes, barriers, terrain, and makeshift weaponry. In addition to assessment skills, CFA also teaches students how to enhance perception and observation skills.

Analysis and Integration Skills

The analytical process is intricately linked to understanding how to defend yourself in any threatening situation. If you want to be the best, every aspect of fighting and personal protection must be dissected. Every strategy, tactic, movement, and concept must be broken down to its atomic parts. The three planes (physical, mental, spiritual) of self-defense must be unified scientifically through arduous practice and constant exploration.

CFA's most advanced practitioners have sound insight and understanding of a wide range of sciences and disciplines. They include human anatomy, kinesiology, criminal justice, sociology, kinesics, proxemics, combat physics, emergency medicine, crisis

The 10 Best Ways to Defeat Multiple Attackers

management, histrionics, police and military science, the psychology of aggression, and the role of archetypes.

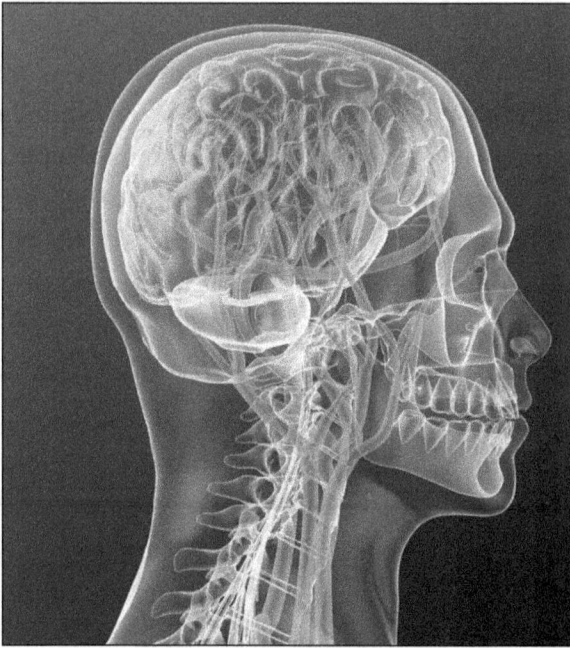

CFA's mental component focuses on the cognitive development of a fighter, including strategic/tactical awareness, analysis and integration, cognitive skills, the killer instinct, and philosophy.

Analytical exercises are also a regular part of CFA training. For example, we conduct problem-solving sessions involving particular assailants attacking in defined environments. We move hypothetical attackers through various ranges to provide insight into tactical solutions. We scrutinize different methods of attack for their general utility in combat. We also discuss the legal ramifications of self-defense on a frequent basis.

In addition to problem-solving sessions, students are slowly exposed to concepts of integration and modification. Oral and written examinations are given to measure intellectual accomplishment. Unlike traditional systems, CFA does not use colored belts or sashes to identify the student's level of proficiency.

Philosophy

Philosophical resolution is essential to a fighter's mental confidence and clarity. Anyone learning the art of war must find the ultimate answers to questions concerning the use of violence in defense of himself or others. To advance to the highest levels of combat awareness, you must find clear and lucid answers to such provocative questions as could you take the life of another, what are your fears, who are you, why are you interested in studying Contemporary Fighting Arts, why are you reading this book, and what is good and what is evil? If you haven't begun the quest to

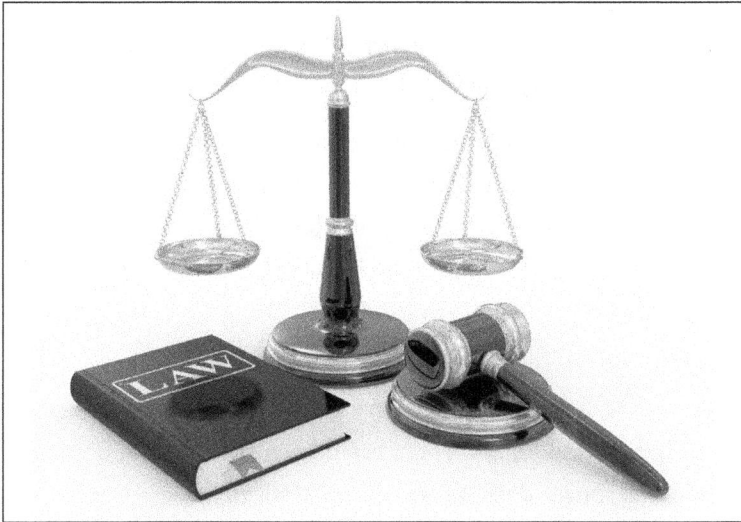

Developing a deadly capability to protect yourself carries tremendous moral and social responsibility. It also involves the risk of civil liability and criminal jeopardy. There is an interesting irony facing most martial artists or self-defense experts. The more highly trained, knowledgeable, and skilled you are in firearms, knives, unarmed combat tactics, martial arts, and other self-defense skills, the higher the standards of care you must follow when protecting yourself and others.

formulate these important questions and answers, then take a break. It's time to figure out just why you want to know the laws and rules of destruction.

Cognitive Combat Skills

Cognitive combat exercises are also important for improving one's fighting skills. CFA uses visualization and crisis rehearsal scenarios to improve general body mechanics, tools and techniques, and maneuvers, as well as tactic selection. Mental clarity, concentration, and emotional control are also developed to enhance one's ability to call upon the controlled killer instinct.

The Spiritual Component

There are many tough fighters out there. In fact, they reside in every town in every country. However, most are nothing more than vicious animals that lack self-mastery. And self-mastery is what separates the true warrior from the eternal novice.

I am not referring to religious precepts or beliefs when I speak of CFA's spiritual component. Unlike most martial arts, CFA does not merge religion into its spiritual aspect. Religion is a very personal and private matter and should never, be incorporated into any fighting system.

CFA's spiritual component is not something that is taught or studied. Rather, it is that which transcends the physical and mental aspects of being and reality. There is a deeper part of each of us that is a tremendous source of truth and accomplishment.

In CFA, the spiritual component is something that is slowly and progressively acquired. During the challenging quest of combat training, one begins to tap the higher qualities of human nature. Those elements of our being that inherently enable us to know right from wrong and good from evil. As we slowly develop this aspect of our total self, we begin to strengthen qualities profoundly important to the "truth." Such qualities are essential to your growth through the mastery of inner peace, the clarity of your "vision," and your recognition of universal truths.

While there are many dedicated individuals who are more than qualified to teach unique philosophical and spiritual components of ancient martial arts, you must realize that such forms of combat can get you killed in a real life self-defense encounter.

One of the goals of my system is to promote virtue and moral responsibility in people who have extreme capacities for physical and mental destructiveness. The spiritual component of fighting is truly the most difficult aspect of personal growth. Yet, unlike the physical component, where the practitioner's abilities will be limited to some degree by genetics and other natural factors, the spiritual component of combat offers unlimited potential for growth and development. In the final analysis, CFA's spiritual component poses the greatest challenges for the student. It is an open-ended plane of unlimited advancement.

The 10 Best Ways to Defeat Multiple Attackers

Chapter One
Getting Ready

The 10 Best Ways to Defeat Multiple Attackers

The Elements of Unarmed Combat

In order to benefit from the information discussed in the next chapter, it's important to have a grasp of the following elements of fighting. They are:

- The Fighting Stance
- Fighting Ranges/ Range Proficiency
- Footwork and Mobility
- Combat Attributes
- Natural Body Weapons
- Anatomical Targets
- Probable Reaction Dynamics

The Fighting Stance

The fighting stance defines your ability to execute both explosive punches and defensive techniques, and it will play a material role in the outcome of any fight. It stresses strategic soundness and simplicity over complexity and style. The fighting stance also facilitates optimum execution of your power punches, while simultaneously protecting your vital targets against quick counter strikes.

The fighting stance is designed around the centerline. The centerline is an imaginary vertical line running through the center of the body, from the top of your head to the bottom of the groin. Most of your vital targets are situated along this line, including the head, throat, solar plexus, and groin. Obviously, you want to avoid directly exposing your centerline to the assailant. To achieve this, position your feet and body at a 45-degree angle from the opponent. This moves your body targets back and away from direct strikes but leaves you strategically positioned to attack.

The right lead fighting stance.   *The left lead fighting stance.*

How to Assume a Fighting Stance

When assuming your fighting stance, place your feet about shoulder width apart. Keep your knees bent and flexible. Think of your legs as power springs to launch you through the ranges of unarmed combat (kicking, punching, and grappling range).

Mobility is also important, as we'll discuss later. All footwork and strategic movement should be performed on the balls of your feet. Your weight distribution is also an important factor. Since combat is dynamic, your weight distribution will frequently change. However, when stationary, keep 50 percent of your body weight on each leg and always be in control of it.

The hands are aligned one behind the other along your centerline.

The lead arm is held high and bent at approximately 90 degrees. The rear arm is kept back by the chin. Arranged this way, the hands not only protect the upper centerline but also allow quick deployment of your body weapons. When holding your guard, do not tighten your shoulder or arm muscles prior to striking. Stay relaxed and loose. Finally, keep your chin slightly angled down. This diminishes target size and reduces the likelihood of a paralyzing blow to your chin or a lethal strike to your throat.

A solid fighting stance must be maintained when executing combat techniques. Pictured here, the author (right) maintains the proper hand guard position during the execution of his kick.

The best method for practicing your fighting stance is in front of a full-length mirror. Place the mirror in an area that allows sufficient room for movement; a garage or basement is perfect. Stand in front of the mirror, far enough away to see your entire body. Stand naturally with your arms relaxed at your sides. Now close your eyes and quickly assume your fighting stance. Open your eyes and check for flaws.

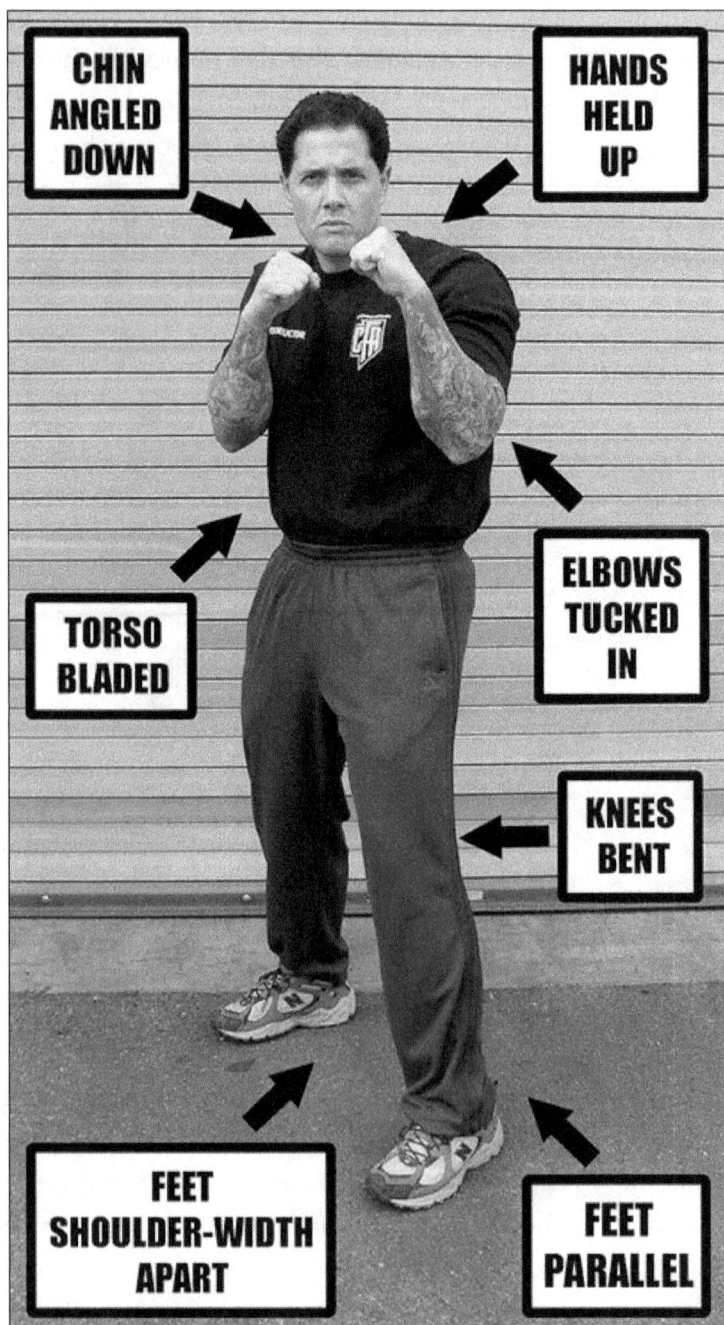

Look for low hand guards, improper foot positioning or body angle, rigid shoulders and knees, etc. Drill this way repeatedly, working from both the right and left side. Practice this until your fighting stance becomes second nature.

Fighting Stance Drill (Shadow Fighting)

Shadow fighting is another exercises you can do to improve your fighting stance. Essentially, shadow fighting is the creative deployment of offensive and defensive tools and maneuvers against imaginary assailants from the reference point of a fighting stance.

Shadow fighting requires intense mental concentration, honest self-analysis, and a deep commitment to improve. For those of you on a tight budget, the good news is that shadow fighting is inexpensive. All you need is a full-length mirror and a place to work out. The mirror is vital. It functions as a critic, your personal instructor. If you're honest, the mirror will be too. It will point out every mistake - poor stance structure, telegraphing, sloppy footwork, poor body mechanics, and even lack of physical conditioning.

Proper shadow fighting develops speed, power, balance, footwork, compound attack skills, sound form, and finesse. It even promotes a better understanding of the ranges of combat. As you progress, you can incorporate light dumbbells into shadow fighting workouts to enhance power and speed. Start off with one to three pounds and gradually work your way up. A weight vest can also be worn to develop powerful footwork, kicks, and knee strikes.

If you want to make your fighting stance instinctual, practice it in a slow and controlled fashion with your eyes closed. Closing your eyes when training will help you develop a complete kinesthetic feel for the movement.

The fighting stance is also used as a reference point when training. Here, a student prepares to throw a kick from a fighting stance position.

When shadow fighting be especially aware of the following:

1. Dropping your hands down.

2. Lifting your chin up.

3. Elbows flaring out to the sides.

4. Tensing your muscles before, during and after technique deployment.

5. Unnecessary widening of your feet.

6. Cross stepping when moving sideways.

7. Failing to maintain a 45-degree angle stance.

8. Excessive weight distribution.

The Fighting Ranges and Range Proficiency

Real fighting seldom takes place at a predetermined distance. It can also happen anytime and anywhere. If you want to be prepared to handle any type of combat situation, you'd better be range proficient. Range proficiency is the skill and ability to fight your adversary in all three distances of unarmed combat (kicking range, punching range, and grappling range).

This means that you are capable of fighting an opponent in all possible situations. For example, can you fight an assailant on a bus, in a crowded bar? While lying in your bed or sitting in your car? Do you have the skill to strike an assailant standing five feet away from you? These and other questions pertain to range proficiency.

In unarmed combat, there are only three possible distances from which you can engage your opponent: kicking range, punching range, and grappling range.

Let's start with the kicking range.

Kicking Range

At this distance, you are usually too far to make contact with your hands, so you would use your legs to strike your assailant. For self-defense, you should only employ low-line kicks. These are directed to targets below the assailant's waist, such as the groin, thigh, knee joint, and shin. As a result, I teach my students to use kicking range tools like the vertical, push, side, and hook kicks. They are safe, efficient, and destructive.

The Kicking Range.

Punching Range

This is the midrange of unarmed combat. At this distance, you are close enough to the opponent to strike him with your hands. Hand strikes do not require as much room as kicking, and the surface area that you are standing on is not as crucial a concern.

Effective punching range techniques include the following:: finger jabs, palm heels, knife hands, lead straights, rear crosses, horizontal and shovel hooks, uppercuts, and hammer fists.

The Punching Range.

Grappling Range

The third and closest range of unarmed combat is grappling range. At this distance, you are too close to your opponent to kick or execute some hand strikes, so you would use close-quarter tools and techniques to neutralize your adversary.

Grappling range is divided into two different planes: vertical and horizontal. In the vertical plane, you would deliver impact techniques, some of which include elbow and knee strikes, head butts, gouging and crushing tactics, and biting and tearing techniques.

In the horizontal plane, you are ground fighting with your enemy and can deliver all of the previously mentioned techniques, including various submission holds, locks, and chokes.

The 10 Best Ways to Defeat Multiple Attackers

Pictured here, vertical grappling range.

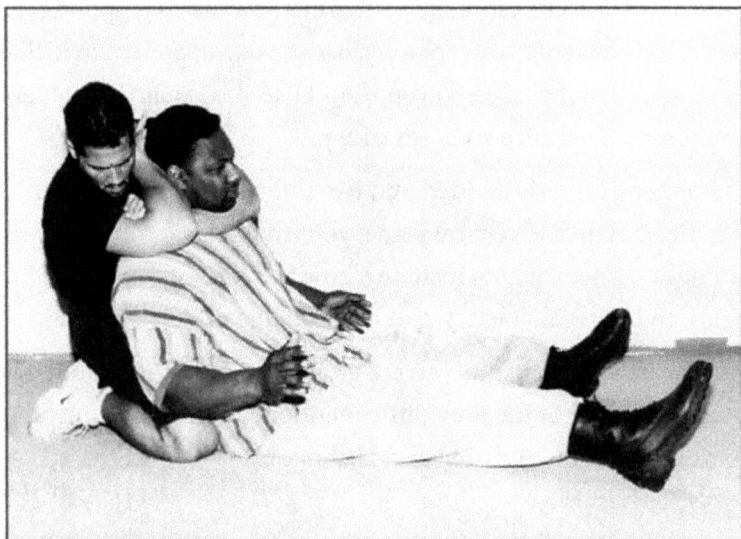

The grappling range (horizontal plane) of unarmed combat. Also known as ground fighting.

Footwork & Mobility

Next are footwork and mobility. I define mobility as the ability to move your body quickly and freely, which is accomplished through basic footwork. The safest footwork involves quick, economical steps performed on the balls of your feet, while you remain relaxed and balanced. Keep in mind that balance is your most important consideration.

Basic footwork can be used for both offensive and defensive purposes, and it is structured around four general directions: forward, backward, right, and left. However, always remember this footwork rule of thumb: Always move the foot closest to the direction you want to go first, and let the other foot follow an equal distance. This prevents cross-stepping, which can cost you your life in a fight.

Basic Footwork Movements

1. Moving forward (advance) - from your fighting stance, first move your front foot forward (approximately 12 inches) and then move your rear foot an equal distance.

2. Moving backward (retreat) - from your fighting stance, first move your rear foot backward (approximately 12 inches) and then move your front foot an equal distance.

3. Moving right (sidestep right) - from your fighting stance, first move your right foot to the right (approximately 12 inches) and then move your left foot an equal distance.

4. Moving left (sidestep left) - from your fighting stance, first move your left foot to the left (approximately 12 inches) and then move your right foot an equal distance.

Practice these four movements for 10 to 15 minutes a day in front of a full-length mirror. In a couple weeks, your footwork should be quick, balanced, and natural.

Circling Right and Left

Strategic circling is an advanced form of footwork where you will use your front leg as a pivot point. This type of movement can also be used defensively to evade an overwhelming assault or to strike the opponent from various strategic angles. Strategic circling can be performed from either a left or right stance.

Circling left (from a left stance) - this means you'll be moving your body around the opponent in a clockwise direction. From a left stance, step 8 to 12 inches to the left with your left foot, then use your left leg as a pivot point and wheel your entire rear leg to the left until the correct stance and positioning is acquired.

Circling right (from a right stance) - from a right stance, step 8 to 12 inches to the right with your right foot, then use your right leg as a pivot point and wheel your entire rear leg to the right until the correct stance and positioning is acquired.

Combat Attributes

A kick, punch, block, or any fighting technique for that matter is useless unless it is accompanied by certain combative attributes. Attributes are qualities that enhance your particular body weapon or technique.

For example, speed, power, timing, non telegraphic movement, rhythm, coordination, accuracy, balance, and range specificity are just a few self-defense attributes that must be present if any technique or maneuver is to be effective in a high-risk self-defense situation.

Let's explore a few basic attributes necessary for fighting: speed, power, timing, balance, and non telegraphic movement.

Speed

To effectively land any offensive strike you must possess speed. By speed, I am referring to how fast your body weapon moves to its target. A fast technique should be likened to the strike of a snake. It should be felt and not seen by your assailant.

While some athletes are blessed with great speed, you should make every possible attempt to develop your speed to the maximum of your ability. One of the easiest ways of enhancing your speed is to simply relax your body prior to executing your body weapon. For example, when executing a palm heel strike to your assailant's chin, your arm should simply shoot straight out and back to its starting point without muscular tension. This may sound simple, but you'd be amazed how many people have difficulty relaxing—especially when they are under tremendous stress. Another way of developing blinding speed is to practice throwing all of your offensive weapons in the air. Focus on quickly executing and retracting your tool or technique as quickly as you can. If you are persistent and work diligently, you can achieve significant results.

Power

Power refers to the amount of impact force you can generate when striking your target. The power of your natural body weapon is not necessarily predicated on your size and strength. A relatively small person can generate devastating power if he or she combines it with sufficient speed. This explains why someone like Bruce Lee who weighed approximately 130 pounds could hit harder than most 200-pound men. Lee knew how to maximize his impact power through the speed at which he executed his techniques.

Ideally, when attempting to strike your assailant, you want to put your entire body behind your blow. I instruct my students to always aim 3 inches through their chosen target. Torquing your hips and shoulder into your blows will also help generate tremendous power. Remember, in a real self-defense situation, you want to hit your assailant with the power equivalent of a shotgun and not a squirt gun.

Timing

Timing refers to your ability to execute a technique or movement at the optimum moment. There are two types of timing: defensive and offensive. Defensive timing is the time between the assailant's attack and your defensive response to that attack. Offensive timing is the time between your recognition of a target opening and your offensive response to that opening.

Among the best ways of developing both offensive and defensive timing are stick and knife fighting, sparring sessions, double-end bag training, and various focus mitt drills. Mental visualization is also another effective method of enhancing timing. Visualizing various self-defense scenarios that require precise timing is ideal for enhancing your skills.

Balance

Effectively striking your assailant requires substantial follow-through while maintaining your balance. Balance is your ability to maintain equilibrium while stationary or moving. You can maintain perfect balance only through controlling your center of gravity, mastering body mechanics, and proper skeletal alignment.

To develop your sense of balance, perform your body weapons and techniques slowly so you become acquainted with the different weight distributions, body positions, and mechanics of each particular weapon. For example, when executing an elbow strike, keep your head, torso, legs, and feet in proper relation to each other. Be certain to follow through your target, but don't overextend yourself.

Non Telegraphic Movement

The element of surprise is an invaluable tool for self-defense. Successfully landing a blow requires that you do not forewarn your assailant of your intentions. Clenching your teeth, widening your eyes, cocking your fist, and tensing your neck or shoulders are just a few common telegraphic cues that will negate the element of surprise.

One of the best ways to prevent telegraphic movement is to maintain a poker face prior to executing your body weapon or technique. Avoid all facial expressions when faced with a threatening assailant. As mentioned, you can study your techniques and maneuvers in front of a full-length mirror or have a friend videotape you performing your movements. These procedures will assist you in identifying and ultimately eliminating telegraphic movements. Be patient and you'll reach your objective.

Natural Body Weapons for Striking

If you want to be able to apply the different fighting methods discussed in the next chapter, you must have a working knowledge of your natural body weapons. Body weapons are simply the various parts of your body that can be used as weapons to neutralize your opponent.

Actually, you have 14 natural body weapons at your immediate disposal. They are easy to learn and, when properly executed, have the potential to disable, cripple, and even kill an attacker. They include the head, teeth, voice, elbows, fists, palms, fingers and nails, edge of hand, web of the hand, knees, shins, dorsum of the foot, heel of foot, and ball of foot.

Let's start with the head.

Head

When you are fighting in close quarters, your head can be used for butting your assailant's nose. Head butts are ideal when a strong attacker has placed you in a hold where your arms are pinned against your sides. Keep in mind that the head butt can be delivered in four different directions: forward, backward, right side, and left side.

Teeth

The teeth can be used for biting anything on the assailant's body (nose, ears, throat, fingers, etc.). It is important, however, for you to muster the mental determination to bite deep and hard into the assailant's flesh and shake your head vigorously, much like a vicious dog killing his enemy. While this may seem primitive and barbaric, it is essential to your survival.

Although a bite is extremely painful, it also transmits a strong psychological message to your assailant. It lets him know that you, too, can be vicious and are willing to do anything to survive the encounter.

Warning: There is one important concern to biting tactics: you run the risk of contracting AIDS if your attacker is infected and you draw blood while biting him.

Elbows

With very little training, you can learn to use your elbows as devastating self-defense weapons. They are explosive, deceptive, and difficult to stop. By rotating your body into the blow, you can generate tremendous force. You can deliver elbow strikes horizontally, vertically, and diagonally to the assailant's nose, temple, chin, throat, solar plexus, and ribs.

Fists

The fists are used for punching an assailant's temple, nose, chin, throat, solar plexus, ribs, and groin. However, punching with your fists is a true art, requiring considerable time and training to master. Punching techniques include the lead straight, rear cross, hooks, upper cuts, shovel hooks, and hammer fists.

Fingers/Nails

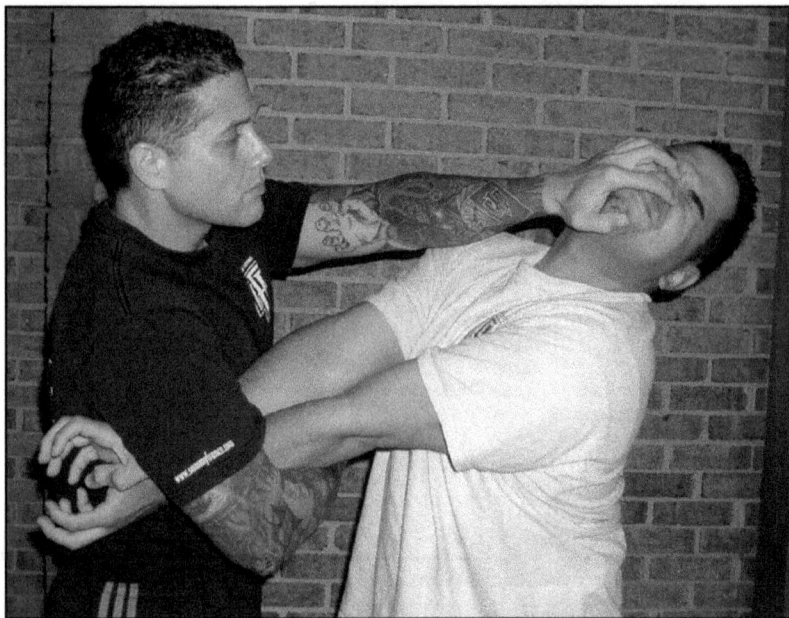

Your fingers and nails can be used for jabbing, gouging, and clawing the opponent's eyes. They can also be used for grabbing, pulling, tearing, and crushing his throat or testicles.

Palms

One alternative to punching with your fists is to strike with the heel of your palm. A palm strike from either one of your hands is very powerful and should always be delivered in an upward, thrusting motion to the assailant's nose or chin.

Edge of the Hand

You can throw the edge of your hand in a whiplike motion to surprise and neutralize your attacker. By whipping your arm horizontally to his nose or throat, you can cause severe injury or death. The edge of your hand can also be thrown vertically or diagonally to the back of the assailant's neck as a finishing blow.

Web of the Hand

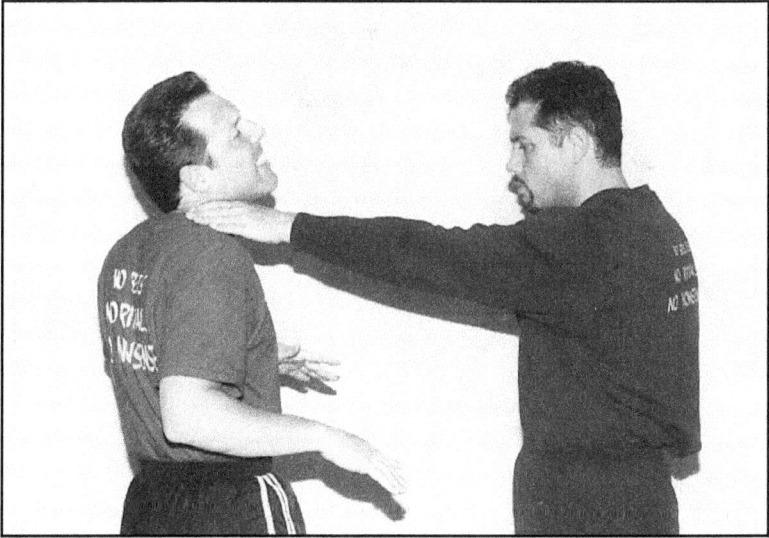

The web of your hand can be used to deliver web hand strikes to the opponent's throat. When striking, be certain to keep your hand stiff with your palm facing down.

Knees

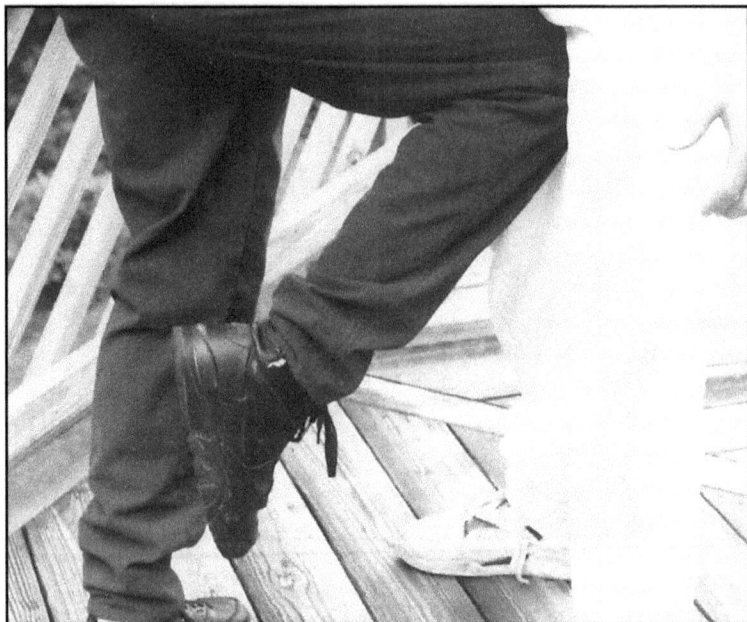

When you are fighting the opponent in close-quarter grappling range, your knees can be extremely powerful weapons. You can deliver knee strikes vertically and diagonally to the assailant's thigh and groin, ribs, solar plexus, and face.

Shins

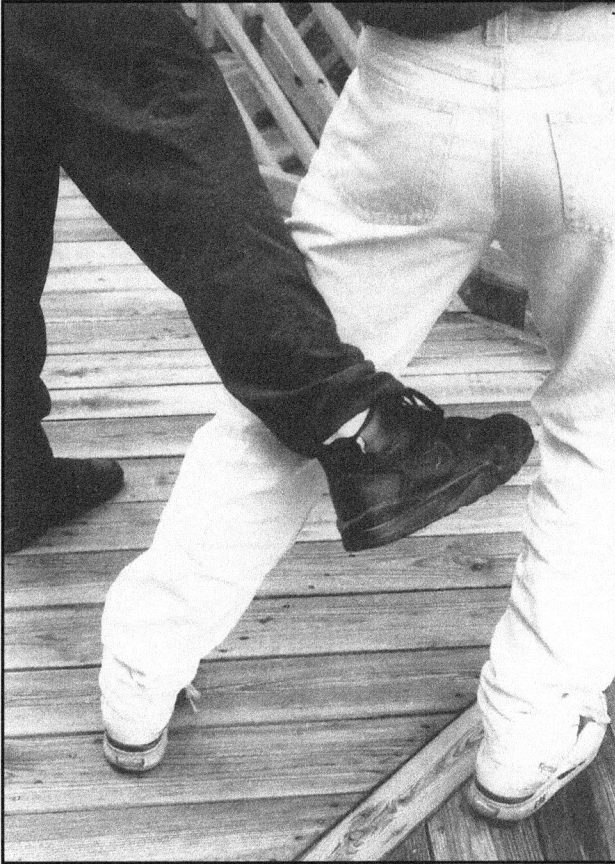

Striking with your shinbone can quickly cripple a powerful assailant and bring him to his knees in agony. That's right—your shinbone is a weapon. When striking with your shin, you can aim for his thigh, the side of his knee, or groin—and always remember to aim through your target.

Dorsum of Foot

You can use the dorsum of your foot to execute a vertical kick to the assailant's groin, and in some cases, his head. Striking with the dorsum increases the power of your kick, prevents broken toes, and also lengthens the surface area of your strike.

Heel of Foot

You can use the heel of your foot to execute a side kick to the opponent's knee or shin. When fighting an attacker in grappling range, you can use the heel of your foot to stomp down on the assailant's instep or toes.

Ball of Foot

You can use the ball of your foot to execute a push kick into the assailant's thigh. You can also snap it quickly into the assailant's shin to loosen a grab from the front. When striking the assailant with the ball of your foot, be certain to pull your toes back to avoid jamming or breaking them.

Anatomical Targets

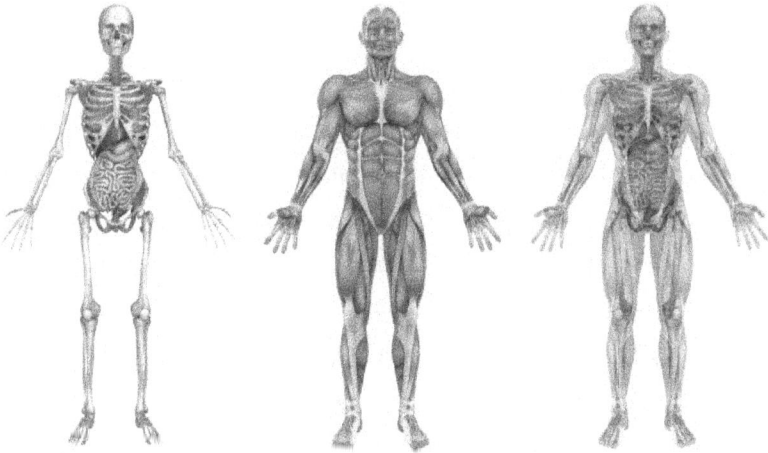

Knowing how and when to strike your opponent is essential; however knowing where to hit him is equally important. Anyone who is seriously interested in neutralizing a formidable adversary must have a working knowledge and understanding of the body targets on the human anatomy. This is called target orientation.

Many people don't realize that the human body has many structural weaknesses that are especially vulnerable to attack. The human body simply was not designed to take the punishment of strikes and blows. Always keep in mind that regardless of your attacker's size, strength, or state of mind, he will always have vulnerable targets that can be attacked.

Unfortunately, very little information has been written on anatomical targets and the medical implications of self-defense strikes. Every martial artist, self-defense expert, combat specialist, and law enforcement officer has a moral and legal responsibility to know the medical implications of strikes and techniques. It is your responsibility to know which targets will stun, incapacitate, disfigure,

The 10 Best Ways to Defeat Multiple Attackers

cripple, or kill your assailant. Knowledge of the medical implications will also make you a more efficient technician.

I am astonished by some martial art and self-defense instructors who teach ineffective targets. For example, the biceps, collar bone, kidneys, coronal suture, or Achilles tendon are just a few targets that yield poor results when struck. Such anatomical targets won't neutralize a vicious opponent immediately. In many cases, it will only anger him and provoke him to attack with greater viciousness and determination. Therefore, it is essential that you strike targets that will immediately incapacitate the opponent. Anything less can get you severely injured or killed. Don't forget this point.

For practical purposes you only need to know a handful of anatomical targets. We will focus on 13 vulnerable targets categorized into three zones.

The 3 Target Zones

For reasons of clarity, we can categorize both the primary and secondary anatomical targets into one of three possible zones.

Zone 1 (Head region) consists of targets related to your senses. This includes: the eyes, temples, nose, chin, and back of neck.

Zone 2 (Neck, Torso, Groin) consists of targets related to breathing. This includes: the throat, solar plexus, ribs, and testicles.

Zone 3 (Legs, Feet) consists of targets related to mobility. This includes: the thighs, knees, shins, instep, and toes.

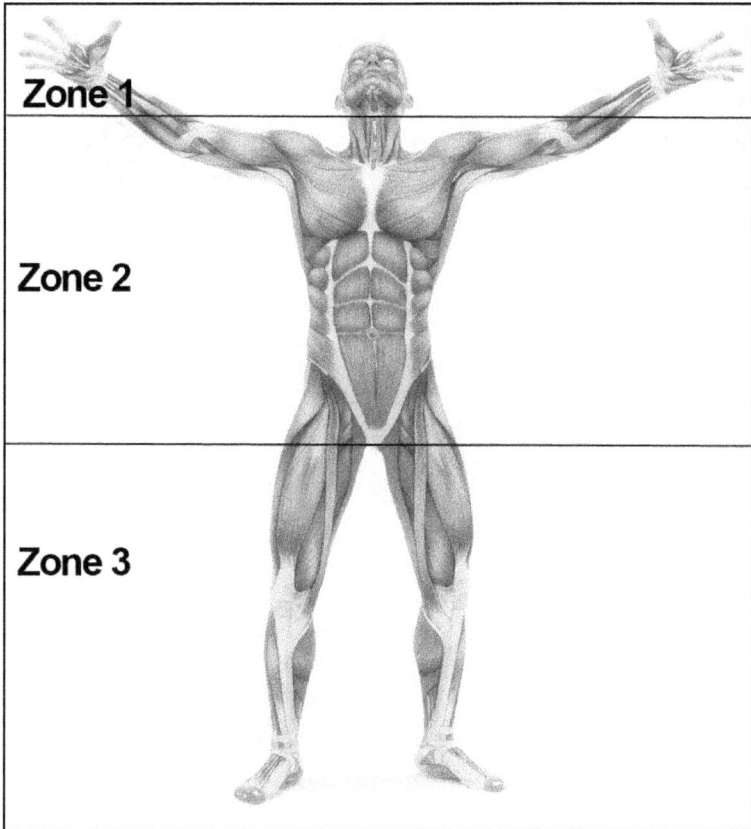

The three target zones.

EYES

Eyes sit in the orbital bones of the skull. They are ideal targets for self-defense because they are extremely sensitive and difficult to protect, and striking them requires very little force. The eyes can be poked, scratched, and gouged from a variety of angles. Depending on the force of your strike, it can cause numerous injuries, including watering of the eyes, hemorrhaging, blurred vision, temporary or permanent blindness, severe pain, rupture, shock, and unconsciousness.

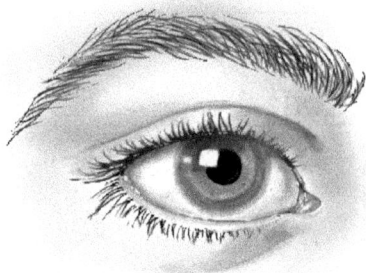

NOSE

The nose is made up of a thin bone, cartilage, numerous blood vessels, and many nerves. It is a particularly good target because it stands out from the opponent's face and can be struck from three different directions (up, straight, down). A moderate blow can cause stunning pain, eye-watering, temporary blindness, and hemorrhaging. A powerful strike can result in shock and unconsciousness.

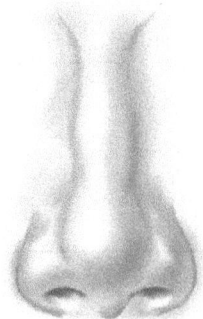

CHIN

In boxing, the chin is considered a "knockout button," responsible for retiring hundreds of boxers. The chin is equally a good target for self-defense. When it is struck at a 45-degree angle, shock is

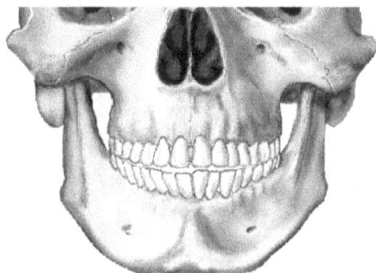

transmitted to the cerebellum and cerebral hemispheres of the brain, resulting in paralysis and immediate unconsciousness. Other possible injuries include broken jaw, concussion, and whiplash to the neck.

TEMPLE

The temple or sphenoid bone is a thin, weak bone located on the side of the skull approximately 1 inch from the eyes. Because of its fragile structure and close proximity to the brain, a powerful strike to this target can be deadly. Other injuries include unconsciousness, hemorrhage, concussion, shock, and coma.

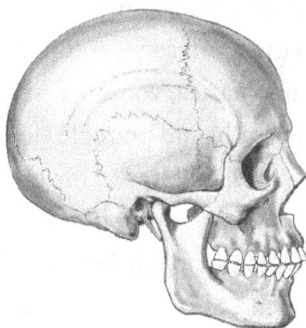

THROAT

The throat is a lethal target because it is only protected by a thin layer of skin. This region consists of the thyroid, hyaline and crocoid cartilage, trachea, and larynx. The trachea, or windpipe, is a cartilaginous tube that measures 4 1/2 inches in length and is approximately 1 inch in diameter. A powerful strike to this target can result in unconsciousness, blood drowning, massive hemorrhaging, air starvation, and death. If the thyroid cartilage is crushed, hemorrhaging will occur, the windpipe will quickly swell shut, resulting in suffocation.

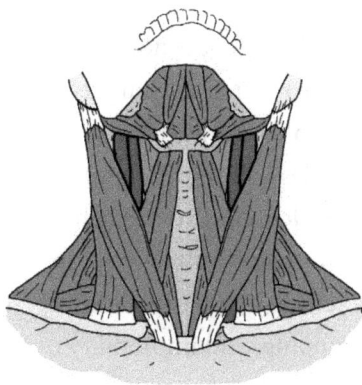

GROIN

Everyone man will agree that the genitals are highly sensitive organs. Even a light strike can be debilitating. A moderate strike to the groin can result in severe pain, nausea, vomiting, shortness of breath, and possible sterility. A powerful blow to the groin can crush the scrotum and testes against the pubic bones, causing shock and unconsciousness.

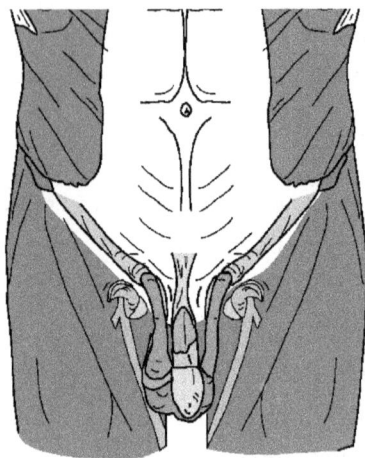

THIGHS

Many people don't realize that the thighs are also vulnerable targets. A moderate kick to the rectus femoris or vastus lateralis muscles will result in immediate immobility of the leg. An extremely hard kick to the thigh can result in a fracture of the femur, resulting in internal bleeding, severe pain, cramping, and immobility of the broken leg.

BACK OF NECK

The back of the neck consists of the first seven vertebrae of the spinal column. They act as a circuit board for nerve impulses from the brain to the body. The back of the neck is a lethal target because the vertebrae are poorly protected. A very powerful strike to the back of the neck can cause shock, unconsciousness, a broken neck, complete paralysis, coma, and death.

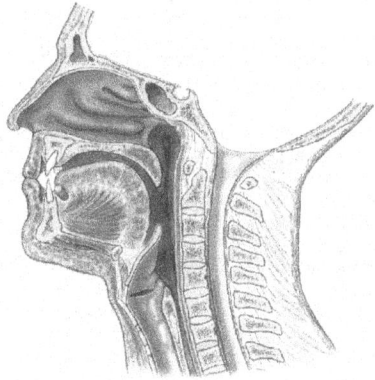

RIBS

There are 12 pair of ribs in the human body. Excluding the eleventh and twelfth ribs, they are long and slender bones that are joined by the vertebral column in the back and the sternum and costal cartilage in the front.

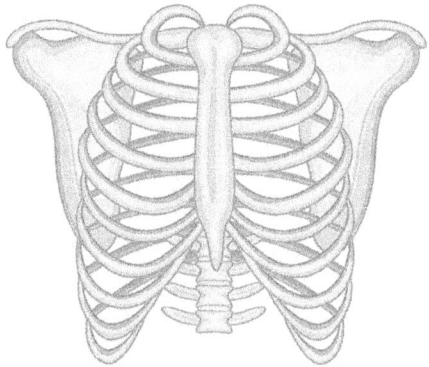

Since there are no eleventh and twelfth ribs (floating ribs) in the front, you should direct your strikes to the ninth and tenth ribs. A moderate strike to the anterior region of the ribs will cause severe pain and shortness of breath. A powerful 45-degree blow could easily break a rib and force it into a lung, resulting in its collapse, internal hemorrhaging, severe pain, air starvation, unconsciousness, and possible death.

SOLAR PLEXUS

The solar plexus is a large collection of nerves situated below the sternum in the upper abdomen. A moderate blow to this area will cause nausea, tremendous pain, and shock, making it difficult for the assailant to breathe. A powerful strike to the solar plexus can result in severe abdominal pain and cramping, air starvation, and shock.

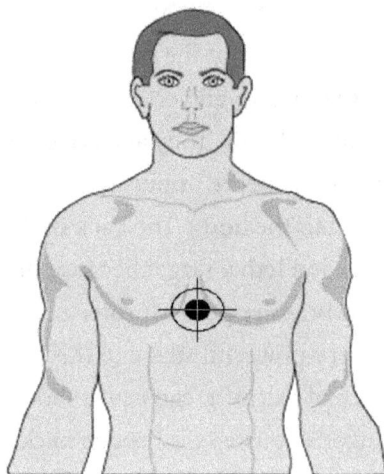

KNEES

The knee connects the femur to the tibia. It is a very weak joint held together by a number of supporting ligaments. When the assailant's leg is locked or fixed and a forceful strike is delivered to the front of the joint, the cruciate ligaments will tear, resulting in excruciating pain, swelling, and immobility.

Located on the front of the knee joint is the patella, which is made of a small, loose piece of bone. The patella is also extremely vulnerable to dislocation by a direct, forceful kick. Severe pain, swelling, and immobility will quickly result.

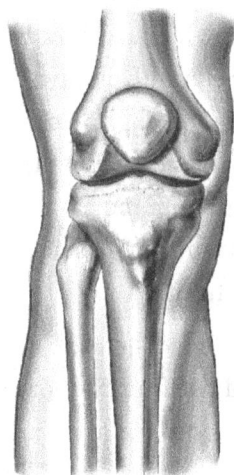

SHINS

Everyone, at one time or another, has knocked his or her shin bone into the end of a table or bed accidentally and felt the intense pain associated with it. The shin is very sensitive because the bone is only protected by a thin layer of skin. However, a powerful kick delivered to this target can easily fracture it, resulting in nauseating pain, hemorrhaging, and immobility.

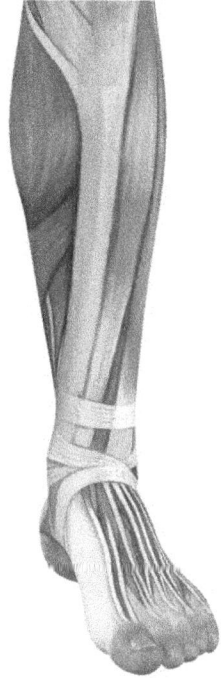

FINGERS

The fingers or digits are considered weak and vulnerable targets that can easily be jammed, sprained, broken, torn, and bitten. While a broken finger might not stop an attacker, it will certainly make him release his hold. A broken finger also makes it difficult for the assailant to clench his fist or hold a weapon. When attempting to break an assailant's finger, it's best to grab the pinkie and forcefully tear backward against the knuckle.

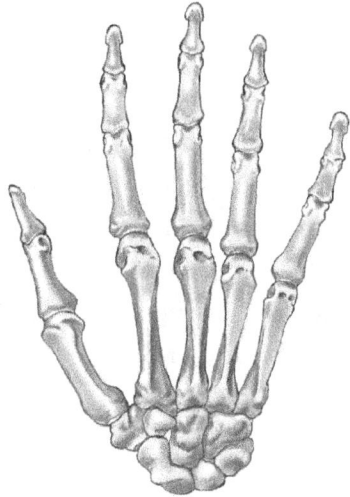

TOES/INSTEP

With a powerful stomp of your heel, you can break the small bones of an assailant's toes and or instep, causing severe pain and immobility. Stomping on the toes is an excellent technique for releasing many holds. It should be mentioned, however, that you should avoid an attack to the toes/instep if the attacker is wearing hard leather boots, i.e., combat, hiking, or motorcycle boots.

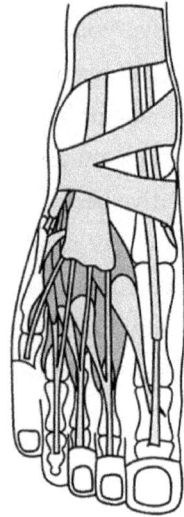

Probable Reaction Dynamics (PRD)

In my book, *Maximum Damage: Hidden Secrets Behind Brutal Fighting Combinations*, I define probable reaction dynamics as the opponent's anticipated or predicted movements or actions that occur in both armed and unarmed combat. Probable reaction dynamics will always be the result or residual of your initial action, i.e., kick, punch, etc.

The most basic example of probable reaction dynamics can be illustrated by the following scenario. Let's say, you deliver a powerful kick to the opponent's groin. When your foot comes in contact with its target, your opponent will exhibit one of several *possible* physical or psychological reactions to your strike. These responses might include:

- The opponent's head and body violently drop forward.

- The opponent grabs or covers his groin region.

- The opponent struggles for breath.

- The opponent momentarily freezes.

- The opponent goes into shock.

Knowledge of your assailant's probable reaction dynamics is vital in all forms of combat, especially when it comes to bar fighting. In fact, you must be mindful of the possible reaction dynamics to every strike, and technique in your arsenal. This is exactly what I refer to as *"reaction dynamic awareness"* and I can assure you this is not such an easy task. However, with regular training, it can be developed.

Just remember, understanding and ultimately mastering reaction dynamic awareness will give you a tremendous advantage in a fight by maximizing the effectiveness, efficiency and safety of your compound attack.

Flow Like Water!

When you proceed with the compound attack, always maintain the offensive flow. The offensive flow is a progression of continuous offensive movements designed to neutralize or, in some cases, terminate your adversary. The key is to have each strike flow smoothly and efficiently from one to the next without causing you to lose ground. Subjecting your adversary to an offensive flow is especially effective because it taxes his nervous system, thereby dramatically lengthening his defensive reaction time.

In a real-life emergency situation it's critical that you always keep the offensive pressure on until your opponent is completely neutralized. Always remember that letting your offensive flow stagnate, even for a second, will open you up to numerous dangers and risks.

Proper breathing is another substantial element of the compound attack, and there is one simple rule that should be followed: exhale during the execution phase of your kick or strike and inhale during its retraction phase. Above all, never hold your breath when delivering several consecutive blows. Doing so could lead to dizziness and fainting, among other complications.

You Don't Have Much Time

Your body can only sustain delivering a compound attack for so long. Initially, your brain will quickly release adrenaline into your blood stream, which will fuel your fighting and enhance your strength and power. This lethal boost of energy is known as an adrenaline dump. However, your ability to exert and maintain this maximum effort will last no more than 30 to 60 seconds if you are in above-average shape. If the fight continues after that, your strength and speed may drop by as much as 50 percent below normal. When all is said and done, you don't have much time in a fight, so the battle needs to be won fast before your energy runs out!

Don't Forget To Relocate!

Subsequent to your compound attack, immediately move to a new location by flanking your adversary. This tactic is known as relocating. Based on the principles of strategy, movement, and surprise, relocating dramatically enhances your safety by making it difficult for your adversary to identify your position after you have attacked him. Remember, if your opponent doesn't know exactly where you are, he won't be able to effectively counterattack.

Actuate Recovery Breathing

Implementing an explosive compound attack will often leave you winded. Because of the volatile nature of street combat, even highly conditioned fighters will show signs of oxygen debt. Hence it's important to employ recovery breathing, the active process of quickly restoring your breathing to its normal state. It requires taking long, deep breaths in a controlled rhythm while avoiding rapid, short gasping. Wind sprints are great for improving your recovery breathing. Consider adding them to your regular training program.

The 10 Best Ways to Defeat Multiple Attackers

Chapter Two

The 10 Best Ways to Defeat Multiple Attackers

You Can Defeat Multiple Attackers!

Defending against multiple attackers is a difficult and treacherous task. The fact is the odds are heavily against you, but you can survive such a confrontation by applying knowledge, skill, training, and raw courage.

Two Types of Multiple Attacker Scenarios

Before moving forward, it's important to understand the two different types of multiple attacker scenarios. They are:

The Ambush

The victim is caught off guard and ambushed by his attackers. One of the best defenses for this type of attack is developing a strong sense of situational awareness. Situational awareness is total alertness, presence, and focus on virtually everything in your immediate surroundings. Situational awareness requires you to detect and assess the people, places, objects, and actions that can pose a danger to you.

The Set-Up

The victim is first approached by the attackers and set-up for the attack. Usually there is some brief dialogue between the attackers and the victim. The set-up differs from the ambush because it offers you greater control of the situation. In fact, your survivability improves significantly because you have more options, tactics, techniques, and strategies at your disposal.

Step 1: Pictured here, the beginning stages of a multiple attacker ambush.

Step 2: The trap is set and the defender walls right into the ambush zone.

Step 3: At this point, the defender is swarmed by his attackers.

Pictured here, the second type of a multiple attacker situation, the Set-Up.

Preparing for the Set-Up

Therefore, this book is going to focus exclusively on defending against a Set-Up multiple attacker situation. The following ten strategic principles will significantly help you if ever you are faced with such a dangerous situation. Finally, keep in mind that in order for them to be effective you must implement them within seconds and without hesitation.

1. Look For Escape Routes or Barriers

When faced with multiple attackers, quickly scan your environment and look for any possible escape routes. Essentially, escape routes are various avenues or exits that permit you to escape from a threatening individual or situation. Escape routes might include windows, fire escapes, doors, gates, escalators, fences, walls, bridges, staircases, or any other avenue that will allow you to flee quickly and safely from this dangerous altercation. However, make sure that your version of an escape route doesn't lead you into a worse situation.

A barrier is any object that obstructs the attacker's path of attack. At the very least, barriers give you distance and some precious time, and they may give you some safety—at least temporarily. A barrier must have the structural integrity to perform the particular function you have assigned it. Barriers are everywhere and include such things as large desks, doors, automobiles, Dumpsters, large trees, fences, walls, heavy machinery, and large vending machines. The list is endless and depends on the situation, but it is a good idea to assess in advance any possible barriers when entering a potentially hostile or dangerous environment.

How many escape routes do you see in this picture?

2. Run

If the opportunity arises for you to run and escape safely, take it! Don't be a fool by thinking it's cowardly to run away from a dangerous situation. There is nothing cowardly about saving your life. A word of caution! If you attempt to outrun your attackers, be certain that you have the athletic ability to really move—and don't offer them target opportunities in your flight.

3. Look for Makeshift Weapons

If you can't escape the situation, look for any possible makeshift weapons that can drastically turn the odds in your favor. Broken bottles, sticks, pipes, crowbars, and shards of broken glass are excellent equalizers that can quickly and effectively neutralize your assailants. However, make certain that you are proficient with these different types of weapons before attempting to use them against your attackers. Otherwise, your attackers may use them against you and make matters worse. For example, if you are going to protect yourself with a shard of glass or broken bottle, you should be well versed with knife fighting tactics.

Makeshift weapons can be broken down into the following (4) four types:

- **Cutting**
- **Shielding**
- **Distracting**
- **Striking**

Cutting makeshift weapons

These are objects or implements used to stab or slash your assailant. Examples include: utility knives, forks, ice pick, screwdriver, broken glass, straight razor, pen, pencil, large nail, ice scraper, fire poker, crow bar, car keys, pitch fork, shovel, hack saw, knitting needle, spike, hatchet, meat hook, scissors, letter opener, cutting shears, trowel.

Shielding makeshift weapons

These are objects used to shield yourself from attack. Examples of shielding makeshift weapons include the following: briefcases, trash-can lids, bicycles, thick sofa cushions, backpacks, barstools, lawn chairs, drawers, cafeteria trays, suitcases, thick pillows, leather jackets/coats, sleeping bags, motorcycle helmets, small end tables, hubcaps, etc. Once again, be certain that your makeshift weapon has the structural integrity to get the job done effectively.

Distracting makeshift weapons

These are objects that can be thrown into your assailant's face, torso, or legs to temporarily distract him. Generally distracting makeshift weapons are thrown into your assailant's face. Some examples include the following: sunglasses, magazines, car keys, wallets, ashtrays, books, salt shakers, alarm clocks, coins, bottles, bars of soap, shoes, dirt, sand, gravel, rocks, videotapes, small figurines, cassette tapes, watering can, hot liquids, paperweights, pesticide sprays, and oven cleaner spray.

Striking makeshift weapons

These are objects used to strike the assailant. Examples of striking makeshift weapons include sticks, bricks, crowbars, baseball bats, shovels, golf clubs, lamps, books, light chair, pool cues, pipes, heavy flashlights, hammers, binoculars, glass bottles, beer mugs, telephones, tool boxes, briefcases, car doors, canes, walking sticks, automobile, light dumbbells, 2 x 4s, etc.

A wide variety of makeshift weapons that can be useful in a multiple attacker self-defense situation.

Avoid using Flexible Makeshift Weapons

Chains, belts, and other flexible makeshift weapons are risky and ineffective for the following reasons:

- They are generally difficult to control.

- They lack neutralizing force.

- They lack quick retraction.

- They must follow through the complete range of motion to be re-executed.

- They open up your body targets to a variety of possible counters.

- They can get snagged on your assailant's body or limbs and force a "lock-up" situation.

Makeshift Weapon Targets

Knowledge of the various makeshift weapons isn't enough. You must have a foundational understanding of the anatomical targets that are vulnerable to each of the three makeshift weapon classifications.

Cutting weapon targets- Targets include the enemy's ear cavities, eye sockets, temples, base of skull, cervical vertebrae, jugular vein, underside of the chin, carotid artery, subclavian, heart, lungs, wrists, back of knees, Achilles tendons, brachial arteries, radial arteries, third and fourth rib regions, solar plexus, groin, and femoral arteries.

Distracting weapon targets - Targets include the enemy's face and eyes, groin, and legs.

Striking weapon targets - Targets include the enemy's head, throat, back of neck, clavicle, lower back, elbows, hands and forearms, ribs, thighs, and knees.

4. Keep Moving

Whenever faced with multiple assailants; always keep moving. Mobility makes you a difficult target to hit and prevents your assailants from surrounding you. It also enhances the power of your strikes, makes the attackers misjudge your range, and helps you find an open area in which to escape.

When you are moving, take quick and efficient steps, while keeping your knees bent and your weight distributed equally on each leg. Be aware of the surface. You don't want to trip or slip.

I define mobility as the ability to move your body quickly and freely, which is accomplished through basic footwork. The safest footwork involves quick, economical steps performed on the balls of your feet, while you remain relaxed and balanced. Keep in mind that balance is one of the most important considerations when fighting multiple opponents.

Mobility and footwork is vital and it's critical that you always stay on your feet. Avoid going to the ground at all costs! As you can see, it's impossible to fight multiple attackers when you are on the ground.

Basic footwork can be used for both offensive and defensive purposes, and it is structured around four general directions: forward, backward, right, and left. However, always remember this footwork rule of thumb: Always move the foot closest to the direction you want to go first, and let the other foot follow an equal distance. This prevents cross-stepping, which can be disastrous in a high-risk combat situation.

Basic Footwork Movements

Moving forward (advance) - from your fighting stance, first move your front foot forward (approximately 12 inches) and then move your rear foot an equal distance.

Moving backward (retreat) - from your fighting stance, first move your rear foot backward (approximately 12 inches) and then move your front foot an equal distance.

Moving right (sidestep right) - from your fighting stance, first move your right foot to the right (approximately 12 inches) and then move your left foot an equal distance.

Moving left (sidestep left) - from your fighting stance, first move your left foot to the left (approximately 12 inches) and then move your right foot an equal distance.

Practice these four movements for 10 to 15 minutes a day in front of a full-length mirror. In a couple weeks, your footwork should be quick, balanced, and natural.

5. Never Let Yourself Be Surrounded

Never, ever let yourself be surrounded by your attackers. It is impossible to defend yourself in every possible direction all at once. Mobility can help prevent you from being trapped. Constantly angle your body so there is always one assailant between you and the rest of them. Take advantage of your environment by trying to maneuver yourself in strategic positions, such as between parked cars or doorways. This prevents them from utilizing their full strength and can permit you to fight them one at a time.

Some experts advise you to keep your back to the wall to prevent being surrounded. I strongly disagree with this because it inhibits your mobility and limits the body mechanics of your kicks. The wall will also provide a possible striking surface for your assailants to smash your head against.

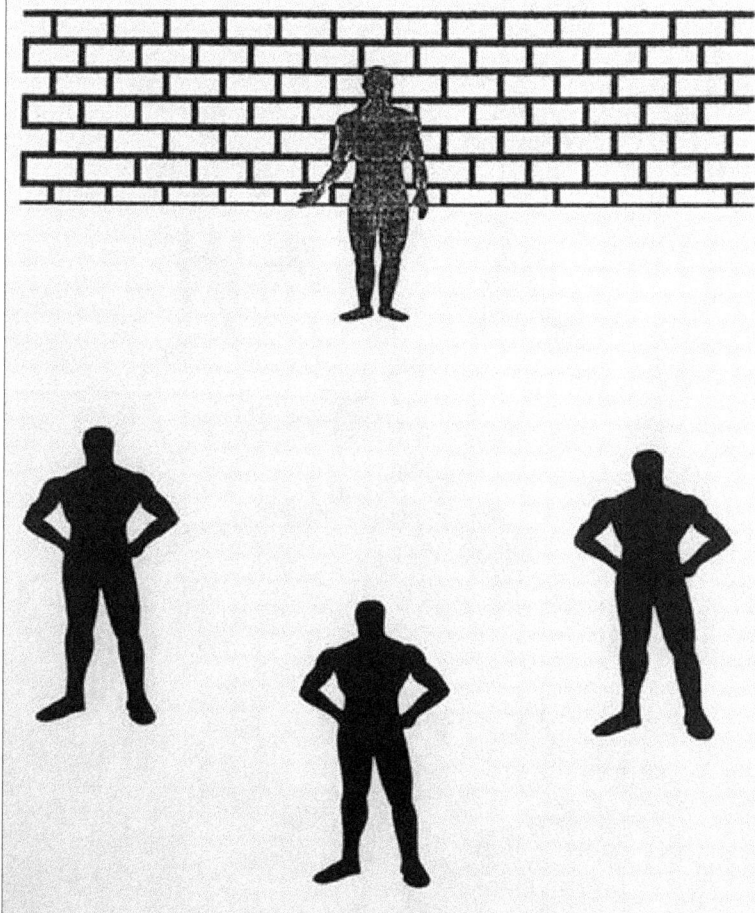

TACTICAL SUICIDE

When fighting multiple attackers, never back yourself into a wall.

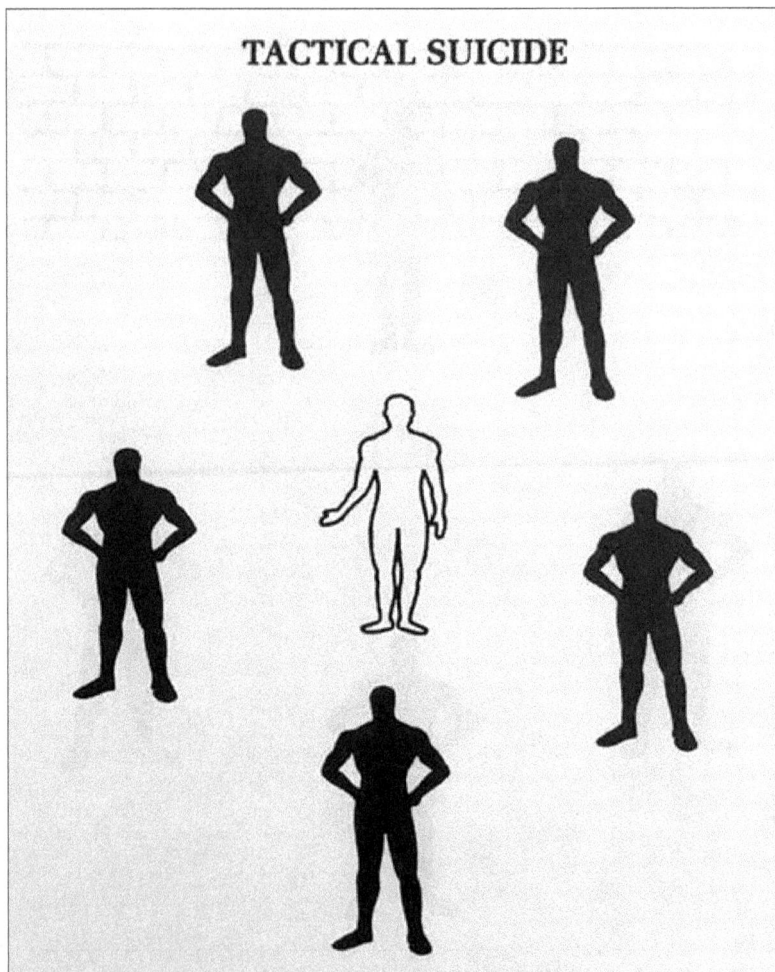

When confronted with multiple assailants, never allow them to surround you. It is physically impossible to protect yourself from all angles.

The dangers of the wall.

6. Assume a Protective Stance

During the pre-contact stages of a group assault, it's important to assume a de-escalation stance. So what is de-escalation and why is it important when defending against multiple attackers? De-escalation is the strategic process of diffusing a potentially violent confrontation. The goal is to eliminate the possibility of agitated individuals resorting to physical violence.

In my Contemporary Fight Arts (CFA) self-defense system, de-escalation is a delicate mixture of science and art, psychology and warfare. It requires you to use both verbal and nonverbal techniques to calm the hostile individuals, while employing tactically deceptive physical safeguards to create the appearance that you are totally non aggressive. It is the art of "tactically calming" the aggressors.

You must be in total control of yourself, both physically and emotionally in order to deal effectively with someone on the verge of losing control. By mastering my de-escalation stance, you will greatly

The 10 Best Ways to Defeat Multiple Attackers

enhance your capability to diffuse the escalating dynamics of a hostile group confrontation.

The Head

When assuming this de-escalation stance, keep your head straight and focused directly at your adversary. Like the fighting stance, you should keep your chin slightly angled down. This diminishes target size and reduces the likelihood of a paralyzing blow to the chin or a lethal strike to the throat. However, it's very important that you appear nonthreatening and non combative to your adversaries.

The Torso

The centerline of your torso should be strategically positioned at a 45-degree angle from your adversary. When assuming the de-escalation stance, place your strongest, most coordinated side forward. For example, a right-handed person stands with his or her right side toward the assailant. Keeping your strongest side forward enhances the speed, power, and accuracy of your first strike. This doesn't mean that you should never practice from your other side. You must be capable of de-escalating from both sides, and you should spend equal practice time on the left and right stances.

The Lead and Rear Arms

Keep your hands open, relaxed and up to protect the upper gates of your centerline. Never drop your hands to your side, put your hands in your pocket, or cross your arms. You've got to have your hands up to strategically protect your anatomical targets and, if necessary, to fight back with your offensive techniques. Don't point your finger or clench your fists! Keep your hands loosely open, both facing the hostile person.

The hands are generally placed one behind the other in a staggered formation along your centerline. The lead arm is held high and bent at approximately 90 degrees. The rear arm is kept back. Arranged this way, the hands not only protect the torso centerline but also allow quick deployment of your body weapons. Finally, when holding your hand guard, do not tighten your shoulder or arm muscle. Stay relaxed and loose.

The Lead and Rear Legs

When assuming your de-escalation stance, place your feet about shoulder width apart. Keep your knees bent and flexible. Your weight distribution is also an important factor. Since self-defense is dynamic, your weight distribution will change frequently. However, when stationary, keep 50 percent of your body weight on each leg and always be in control of it.

When approached by multiple people on the streets, never keep your hands down at your sides.

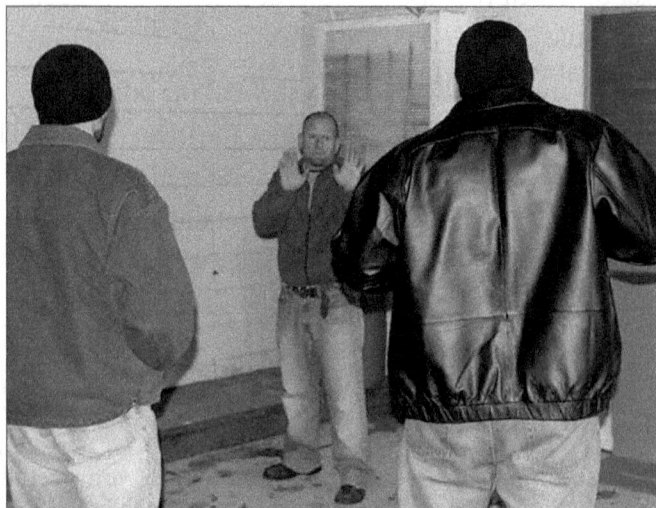

The de-escalation stance is ideal for the pre-contact stages of a group assault because it offers the ability to launch an effective first strike

7. Quickly Determine Which Criminal Is the Immediate Threat

When unarmed and faced with multiple attackers, you must divide them and attack the assailant who presents the most immediate threat to you. Usually the armed assailant is your most immediate threat. If none of the attackers are armed with a weapon, then go for the one closest to you. If more than one attacker is of equal distance from you, then the assailant who is blocking your escape route is the most immediate threat.

Finally, if more than one assailant is blocking your escape route, go for leader or the "alpha" of the group. He's the ringleader who possesses the "spirit of the group" which motivates the others to attack. Also, he's usually the one with the biggest mouth.

When faced with multiple assailants, it's important to quickly determine which one is the immediate threat.

8. Attack Immediate Threat and Make an Example of Your Target

Once you've determined which assailant is the greatest threat, attack him immediately. Quickly move to the flank of the assailant and attack with a barrage of swift blows. Your tactical objective is to injure him as quickly and as efficiently as possible. Remember to strike first, strike fast, strike with authority, and keep the pressure on.

Because of the extreme threat and danger posed by multiple assailants, it is essential to make an example of your target by severely injuring or crippling him. For example, if the others see their buddy violently choking from a vicious throat strike, they will lose spirit and become less inclined to continue their assault on you.

The Two Primary Striking Targets

The two primary anatomical targets to strike in a multiple attacker situation are the eyes and throat. This is not to say that other targets don't matter - they do! However, you should focus your strikes at the eyes and throat because they can instantly disable your attackers. Warning! Always be certain your self-defense actions are legally and morally justified in the eyes of the law!

EYES

Eyes sit in the orbital bones of the skull. They are ideal targets for multiple attackers because they are extremely sensitive and difficult to protect, and damaging them requires very little force. The eyes can be poked, scratched,

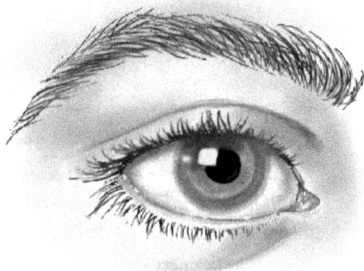

and gouged from a variety of angles. Depending on the force of your strike, it can cause numerous injuries, including:

- watering of the eyes
- hemorrhaging,
- blurred vision
- temporary or permanent blindness
- severe pain
- rupture
- shock
- unconsciousness

Pictured here, the finger jab strike to the eyes.

THROAT

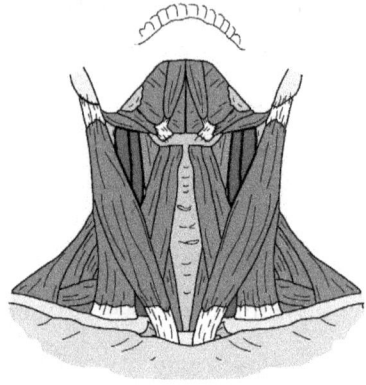

The throat is a lethal razing target because it is only protected by a thin layer of skin. This region consists of the thyroid, hyaline and crocoid cartilage, trachea, and larynx. The trachea, or windpipe, is a cartilaginous tube that measures 4 1/2 inches in length and is approximately 1 inch in diameter. A powerful strike to this target can result in:

- unconsciousness
- blood drowning
- massive hemorrhaging
- air starvation
- death

If the thyroid cartilage is crushed, hemorrhaging will occur, the windpipe will quickly swell shut, resulting in suffocation.

Some effective striking techniques include:

- Finger jab strikes to the eyes.
- Clawing and raking the eyes.
- Web hand strikes to the throat.
- Crushing the opponent's windpipe (only in deadly force self-defense situations).
- Gouging the eyes with both thumbs (if forced into CQC range).

9. Apply the Assembly Line Principle

While you are attacking the immediate threat, try to
maneuver yourself so a straight line is created between you and
all of the attackers. I call this the "assembly line principle" because
it forces assailant number one to be a natural barrier between you
and the other attackers. Once again, this will only buy you a couple
of seconds, but a few precious seconds can make all the difference
between life and death.

Pictured here, the assembly line principle.

The 10 Best Ways to Defeat Multiple Attackers

Step 1: The defender (left) assumes a de-escalation stance and attempts to diffuse the hostile aggressors.

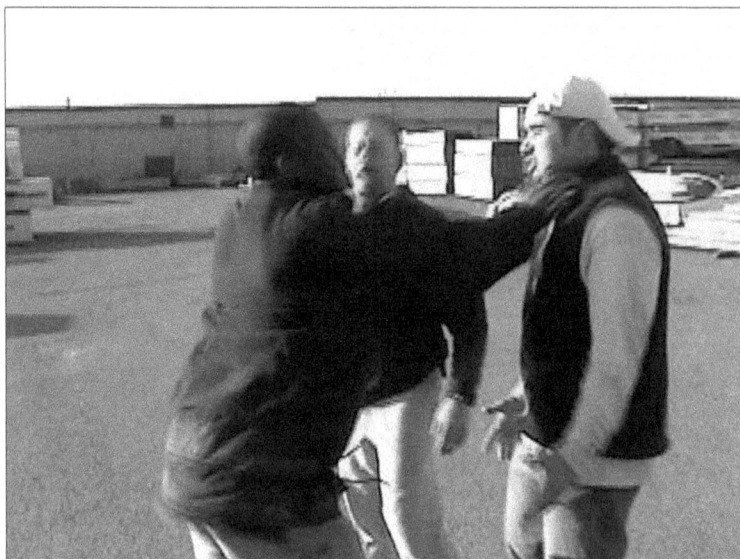

Step 2: The defender determines that danger is imminent and strikes first with a double web hand strike to his attacker's throats.

Step 3: The defender applies the assembly line principle by quickly relocating to the aggressor's flank. If need be, he can continue to strike the nearest aggressor or escape to safety.

10. Apply the Human Shield Principle

Once you've injured the first attacker, use him as an obstacle or "human shield" to the help prevent the other attackers from reaching you. For example, try pushing or swinging him into the other attackers. This will momentarily slow down the other assailants and give you a few seconds to either escape or attack again.

Pictured here, the author (left) applies the human shield principle.

Finally, Don't Stop Fighting Until...

If there still is no opportunity to escape, quickly attack the next assailant. But remember, whenever you decide to fight a group of assailants, you cannot stop fighting until one of the following occurs:

1. Every attacker is neutralized.

2. The other attackers decide to quit.

3. The opportunity to escape safely presents itself.

The 10 Best Ways to Defeat Multiple Attackers

Glossary

The following terms are defined in the context of Contemporary Fighting Arts and its related concepts. In many instances, the definitions bear little resemblance to those found in a standard dictionary.

A

accuracy—The precise or exact projection of force. Accuracy is also defined as the ability to execute a combative movement with precision and exactness.

adaptability—The ability to physically and psychologically adjust to new or different conditions or circumstances of combat.

advanced first-strike tools—Offensive techniques that are specifically used when confronted with multiple opponents.

aerobic exercise—Literally, "with air." Exercise that elevates the heart rate to a training level for a prolonged period of time, usually 30 minutes.

affective preparedness – One of the three components of preparedness. Affective preparedness means being emotionally, philosophically, and spiritually prepared for the strains of combat. See cognitive preparedness and psychomotor preparedness.

aggression—Hostile and injurious behavior directed toward a person.

aggressive response—One of the three possible counters when assaulted by a grab, choke, or hold from a standing position. Aggressive response requires you to counter the enemy with destructive blows and strikes. See moderate response and passive response.

aggressive hand positioning—Placement of hands so as to imply aggressive or hostile intentions.

agility—An attribute of combat. One's ability to move his or her body quickly and gracefully.

amalgamation—A scientific process of uniting or merging.

ambidextrous—The ability to perform with equal facility on both the right and left sides of the body.

anabolic steroids – synthetic chemical compounds that resemble the male sex hormone testosterone. This performance-enhancing drug is known to increase lean muscle mass, strength, and endurance.

analysis and integration—One of the five elements of CFA's mental component. This is the painstaking process of breaking down various elements, concepts, sciences, and disciplines into their atomic parts, and then methodically and strategically analyzing, experimenting, and drastically modifying the information so that it fulfills three combative requirements: efficiency, effectiveness, and safety. Only then is it finally integrated into the CFA system.

anatomical striking targets—The various anatomical body targets that can be struck and which are especially vulnerable to potential harm. They include: the eyes, temple, nose, chin, back of neck, front of neck, solar plexus, ribs, groin, thighs, knees, shins, and instep.

anchoring – The strategic process of trapping the assailant's neck or limb in order to control the range of engagement during razing.

assailant—A person who threatens or attacks another person.

assault—The threat or willful attempt to inflict injury upon the person of another.

assault and battery—The unlawful touching of another person without justification.

assessment—The process of rapidly gathering, analyzing, and accurately evaluating information in terms of threat and danger. You can assess people, places, actions, and objects.

attack—Offensive action designed to physically control, injure, or kill another person.

attack by combination (ABC) - One of the five methods of attack. See compound attack.

attack by drawing (ABD) - One of the five methods of attack. A method of attack predicated on counterattack.

attitude—One of the three factors that determine who wins a street fight. Attitude means being emotionally, philosophically, and spiritually liberated from societal and religious mores. See skills and knowledge.

attributes of combat—The physical, mental, and spiritual qualities that enhance combat skills and tactics.

awareness—Perception or knowledge of people, places, actions, and objects. (In CFA, there are three categories of tactical awareness: criminal awareness, situational awareness, and self-awareness.)

B

balance—One's ability to maintain equilibrium while stationary or moving.

blading the body—Strategically positioning your body at a 45-degree angle.

blitz and disengage—A style of sparring whereby a fighter moves into a range of combat, unleashes a strategic compound attack, and then quickly disengages to a safe distance. Of all sparring methodologies, the blitz and disengage most closely resembles a real street fight.

block—A defensive tool designed to intercept the assailant's attack by placing a non-vital target between the assailant's strike and your vital body target.

body composition—The ratio of fat to lean body tissue.

body language—Nonverbal communication through posture, gestures, and facial expressions.

body mechanics—Technically precise body movement during the execution of a body weapon, defensive technique, or other fighting maneuver.

body tackle – A tackle that occurs when your opponent haphazardly rushes forward and plows his body into yours.

body weapon—Also known as a tool, one of the various body parts that can be used to strike or otherwise injure or kill a criminal assailant.

burn out—A negative emotional state acquired by physically over- training. Some symptoms include: illness, boredom, anxiety, disinterest in training, and general sluggishness.

C

cadence—Coordinating tempo and rhythm to establish a timing pattern of movement.

cardiorespiratory conditioning—The component of physical fitness that deals with the heart, lungs, and circulatory system.

centerline—An imaginary vertical line that divides your body in half and which contains many of your vital anatomical targets.

choke holds—Holds that impair the flow of blood or oxygen to the brain.

circular movements—Movements that follow the direction of a curve.

close-quarter combat—One of the three ranges of knife and

bludgeon combat. At this distance, you can strike, slash, or stab your assailant with a variety of close-quarter techniques.

cognitive development—One of the five elements of CFA's mental component. The process of developing and enhancing your fighting skills through specific mental exercises and techniques. See analysis and integration, killer instinct, philosophy, and strategic/tactical development.

cognitive exercises—Various mental exercises used to enhance fighting skills and tactics.

cognitive preparedness – One of the three components of preparedness. Cognitive preparedness means being equipped with the strategic concepts, principles, and general knowledge of combat. See affective preparedness and psychomotor preparedness.

combat-oriented training—Training that is specifically related to the harsh realities of both armed and unarmed combat. See ritual-oriented training and sport-oriented training.

combative arts—The various arts of war. See martial arts.

combative attributes—See attributes of combat.

combative fitness—A state characterized by cardiorespiratory and muscular/skeletal conditioning, as well as proper body composition.

combative mentality—Also known as the killer instinct, this is a combative state of mind necessary for fighting. See killer instinct.

combat ranges—The various ranges of unarmed combat.

combative utility—The quality of condition of being combatively useful.

combination(s)—See compound attack.

common peroneal nerve—A pressure point area located approximately four to six inches above the knee on the midline of the outside of the thigh.

composure—A combative attribute. Composure is a quiet and focused mind-set that enables you to acquire your combative agenda.

compound attack—One of the five conventional methods of attack. Two or more body weapons launched in strategic succession whereby the fighter overwhelms his assailant with a flurry of full speed, full-force blows.

conditioning training—A CFA training methodology requiring the practitioner to deliver a variety of offensive and defensive combinations for a 4-minute period. See proficiency training and street training.

contact evasion—Physically moving or manipulating your body to avoid being tackled by the adversary.

Contemporary Fighting Arts—A modern martial art and self-defense system made up of three parts: physical, mental, and spiritual.

conventional ground-fighting tools—Specific ground-fighting techniques designed to control, restrain, and temporarily incapacitate your adversary. Some conventional ground fighting tactics include: submission holds, locks, certain choking techniques, and specific striking techniques.

coordination—A physical attribute characterized by the ability to perform a technique or movement with efficiency, balance, and accuracy.

counterattack—Offensive action made to counter an assailant's initial attack.

courage—A combative attribute. The state of mind and spirit that enables a fighter to face danger and vicissitudes with confidence, resolution, and bravery.

creatine monohydrate—A tasteless and odorless white powder that mimics some of the effects of anabolic steroids. Creatine is a safe body-building product that can benefit anyone who wants to increase their strength, endurance, and lean muscle mass.

criminal awareness—One of the three categories of CFA awareness. It involves a general understanding and knowledge of the nature and dynamics of a criminal's motivations, mentalities, methods, and capabilities to perpetrate violent crime. See situational awareness and self-awareness.

criminal justice—The study of criminal law and the procedures associated with its enforcement.

criminology—The scientific study of crime and criminals.

cross-stepping—The process of crossing one foot in front of or behind the other when moving.

crushing tactics—Nuclear grappling-range techniques designed to crush the assailant's anatomical targets.

D

deadly force—Weapons or techniques that may result in unconsciousness, permanent disfigurement, or death.

deception—A combative attribute. A stratagem whereby you delude your assailant.

decisiveness—A combative attribute. The ability to follow a tactical course of action that is unwavering and focused.

defense—The ability to strategically thwart an assailant's attack (armed or unarmed).

defensive flow—A progression of continuous defensive responses.

defensive mentality—A defensive mind-set.

defensive reaction time—The elapsed time between an assailant's physical attack and your defensive response to that attack. See offensive reaction time.

demeanor—A person's outward behavior. One of the essential factors to consider when assessing a threatening individual.

diet—A lifestyle of healthy eating.

disingenuous vocalization—The strategic and deceptive utilization of words to successfully launch a preemptive strike at your adversary.

distancing—The ability to quickly understand spatial relationships and how they relate to combat.

distractionary tactics—Various verbal and physical tactics designed to distract your adversary.

double-end bag—A small leather ball hung from the ceiling and anchored to the floor with bungee cord. It helps develop striking accuracy, speed, timing, eye-hand coordination, footwork and overall defensive skills.

double-leg takedown—A takedown that occurs when your opponent shoots for both of your legs to force you to the ground.

E

ectomorph—One of the three somatotypes. A body type characterized by a high degree of slenderness, angularity, and fragility. See endomorph and mesomorph.

effectiveness—One of the three criteria for a CFA body weapon, technique, tactic, or maneuver. It means the ability to produce a desired effect. See efficiency and safety.

efficiency—One of the three criteria for a CFA body weapon, technique, tactic, or maneuver. It means the ability to reach an objective quickly and economically. See effectiveness and safety.

emotionless—A combative attribute. Being temporarily devoid of human feeling.

endomorph—One of the three somatotypes. A body type characterized by a high degree of roundness, softness, and body fat. See ectomorph and mesomorph.

evasion—A defensive maneuver that allows you to strategically maneuver your body away from the assailant's strike.

evasive sidestepping—Evasive footwork where the practitioner moves to either the right or left side.

evasiveness—A combative attribute. The ability to avoid threat or danger.

excessive force—An amount of force that exceeds the need for a particular event and is unjustified in the eyes of the law.

experimentation—The painstaking process of testing a combative hypothesis or theory.

explosiveness—A combative attribute that is characterized by a sudden outburst of violent energy.

F

fear—A strong and unpleasant emotion caused by the anticipation or awareness of threat or danger. There are three stages of fear in order of intensity: fright, panic, and terror. See fright, panic, and terror.

feeder—A skilled technician who manipulates the focus mitts.

femoral nerve—A pressure point area located approximately 6 inches above the knee on the inside of the thigh.

fighting stance—Any one of the stances used in CFA's system. A strategic posture you can assume when face-to-face with an unarmed assailant(s). The fighting stance is generally used after you have launched your first-strike tool.

fight-or-flight syndrome—A response of the sympathetic nervous system to a fearful and threatening situation, during which it prepares your body to either fight or flee from the perceived danger.

finesse—A combative attribute. The ability to skillfully execute a movement or a series of movements with grace and refinement.

first strike—Proactive force used to interrupt the initial stages of an assault before it becomes a self-defense situation.

first-strike principle—A CFA principle that states that when physical danger is imminent and you have no other tactical option but to fight back, you should strike first, strike fast, and strike with authority and keep the pressure on.

first-strike stance—One of the stances used in CFA's system. A strategic posture used prior to initiating a first strike.

first-strike tools—Specific offensive tools designed to initiate a preemptive strike against your adversary.

fisted blows – Hand blows delivered with a clenched fist.

five tactical options – The five strategic responses you can make in a self-defense situation, listed in order of increasing level of resistance: comply, escape, de-escalate, assert, and fight back.

flexibility—The muscles' ability to move through maximum natural ranges. See muscular/skeletal conditioning.

focus mitts—Durable leather hand mitts used to develop and sharpen offensive and defensive skills.

footwork—Quick, economical steps performed on the balls of the feet while you are relaxed, alert, and balanced. Footwork is structured around four general movements: forward, backward, right, and left.

fractal tool—Offensive or defensive tools that can be used in more than one combat range.

fright—The first stage of fear; quick and sudden fear. See panic and terror.

full Beat – One of the four beat classifications in the Widow Maker Program. The full beat strike has a complete initiation and retraction phase.

G

going postal - a slang term referring to a person who suddenly and unexpectedly attacks you with an explosive and frenzied flurry of blows. Also known as postal attack.

grappling range—One of the three ranges of unarmed combat. Grappling range is the closest distance of unarmed combat from which you can employ a wide variety of close-quarter tools and techniques. The grappling range of unarmed combat is also divided into two planes: vertical (standing) and horizontal (ground fighting). See kicking range and punching range.

grappling-range tools—The various body tools and techniques that are employed in the grappling range of unarmed combat, including head butts; biting, tearing, clawing, crushing, and gouging tactics; foot stomps, horizontal, vertical, and diagonal elbow strikes, vertical and diagonal knee strikes, chokes, strangles, joint locks, and holds. See punching range tools and kicking range tools.

ground fighting—Also known as the horizontal grappling plane, this is fighting that takes place on the ground.

guard—Also known as the hand guard, this refers to a fighter's hand positioning.

guard position—Also known as leg guard or scissors hold, this is a ground-fighting position in which a fighter is on his back holding his opponent between his legs.

H

half beat – One of the four beat classifications in the Widow Maker Program. The half beat strike is delivered through the retraction phase of the proceeding strike.

hand immobilization attack (HIA) - One of the five methods of attack. A method of attack whereby the practitioner traps his opponent's limb or limbs in order to execute an offense attack of his own.

hand positioning—See guard.

hand wraps—Long strips of cotton that are wrapped around the hands and wrists for greater protection.

haymaker—A wild and telegraphed swing of the arms executed by an unskilled fighter.

head-hunter—A fighter who primarily attacks the head.

heavy bag—A large cylindrical bag used to develop kicking, punching, or striking power.

high-line kick—One of the two different classifications of a kick. A kick that is directed to targets above an assailant's waist level. See low-line kick.

hip fusing—A full-contact drill that teaches a fighter to "stand his ground" and overcome the fear of exchanging blows with a stronger opponent. This exercise is performed by connecting two fighters with a 3-foot chain, forcing them to fight in the punching range of unarmed combat.

histrionics—The field of theatrics or acting.

hook kick—A circular kick that can be delivered in both kicking and punching ranges.

hook punch—A circular punch that can be delivered in both the punching and grappling ranges.

I

impact power—Destructive force generated by mass and velocity.

impact training—A training exercise that develops pain tolerance.

incapacitate—To disable an assailant by rendering him unconscious or damaging his bones, joints, or organs.

initiative—Making the first offensive move in combat.

inside position—The area between the opponent's arms, where he has the greatest amount of control.

intent—One of the essential factors to consider when assessing a threatening individual. The assailant's purpose or motive. See demeanor, positioning, range, and weapon capability.

intuition—The innate ability to know or sense something without the use of rational thought.

J

jeet kune do (JKD) - "Way of the intercepting fist." Bruce Lee's approach to the martial arts, which includes his innovative concepts, theories, methodologies, and philosophies.

jersey Pull – Strategically pulling the assailant's shirt or jacket over his head as he disengages from the clinch position.

joint lock—A grappling-range technique that immobilizes the assailant's joint.

K

kick—A sudden, forceful strike with the foot.

kicking range—One of the three ranges of unarmed combat. Kicking range is the furthest distance of unarmed combat wherein you use your legs to strike an assailant. See grappling range and punching range.

kicking-range tools—The various body weapons employed in the kicking range of unarmed combat, including side kicks, push kicks, hook kicks, and vertical kicks.

killer instinct—A cold, primal mentality that surges to your consciousness and turns you into a vicious fighter.

kinesics—The study of nonlinguistic body movement communications. (For example, eye movement, shrugs, or facial gestures.)

kinesiology—The study of principles and mechanics of human movement.

kinesthetic perception—The ability to accurately feel your body during the execution of a particular movement.

knowledge—One of the three factors that determine who will win a street fight. Knowledge means knowing and understanding how to fight. See skills and attitude.

L

lead side -The side of the body that faces an assailant.

leg guard—See guard position.

linear movement—Movements that follow the path of a straight line.

low-maintenance tool—Offensive and defensive tools that require the least amount of training and practice to maintain proficiency. Low maintenance tools generally do not require preliminary stretching.

low-line kick—One of the two different classifications of a kick. A kick that is directed to targets below the assailant's waist level. (See high-line kick.)

lock—See joint lock.

M

maneuver—To manipulate into a strategically desired position.

MAP—An acronym that stands for moderate, aggressive, passive. MAP provides the practitioner with three possible responses to various grabs, chokes, and holds that occur from a standing position. See aggressive response, moderate response, and passive response.

martial arts—The "arts of war."

masking—The process of concealing your true feelings from your opponent by manipulating and managing your body language.

mechanics—(See body mechanics.)

mental attributes—The various cognitive qualities that enhance your fighting skills.

mental component—One of the three vital components of the CFA system. The mental component includes the cerebral aspects of fighting including the killer instinct, strategic and tactical development, analysis and integration, philosophy, and cognitive development. See physical component and spiritual component.

mesomorph—One of the three somatotypes. A body type classified by a high degree of muscularity and strength. The mesomorph possesses the ideal physique for unarmed combat. See ectomorph and endomorph.

mobility—A combative attribute. The ability to move your body quickly and freely while balanced. See footwork.

moderate response—One of the three possible counters when assaulted by a grab, choke, or hold from a standing position. Moderate response requires you to counter your opponent with a control and restraint (submission hold). See aggressive response and passive response.

modern martial art—A pragmatic combat art that has evolved to meet the demands and characteristics of the present time.

mounted position—A dominant ground-fighting position where a fighter straddles his opponent.

muscular endurance—The muscles' ability to perform the same motion or task repeatedly for a prolonged period of time.

muscular flexibility—The muscles' ability to move through maximum natural ranges.

muscular strength—The maximum force that can be exerted by a particular muscle or muscle group against resistance.

muscular/skeletal conditioning—An element of physical fitness that entails muscular strength, endurance, and flexibility.

N

naked choke—A throat choke executed from the chest to back position. This secure choke is executed with two hands and it can be performed while standing, kneeling, and ground fighting with the opponent.

neck crush – A powerful pain compliance technique used when the adversary buries his head in your chest to avoid being razed.

neutralize—See incapacitate.

neutral zone—The distance outside the kicking range at which neither the practitioner nor the assailant can touch the other.

nonaggressive physiology—Strategic body language used prior to initiating a first strike.

nontelegraphic movement—Body mechanics or movements that do not inform an assailant of your intentions.

nuclear ground-fighting tools—Specific grappling range tools designed to inflict immediate and irreversible damage. Nuclear tools and tactics include biting tactics, tearing tactics, crushing tactics, continuous choking tactics, gouging techniques, raking tactics, and all striking techniques.

O

offense—The armed and unarmed means and methods of attacking a criminal assailant.

offensive flow—Continuous offensive movements (kicks, blows, and strikes) with unbroken continuity that ultimately neutralize or terminate the opponent. See compound attack.

offensive reaction time—The elapsed time between target selection and target impaction.

one-mindedness—A state of deep concentration wherein you are free from all distractions (internal and external).

ostrich defense—One of the biggest mistakes one can make when defending against an opponent. This is when the practitioner looks away from that which he fears (punches, kicks, and strikes). His mentality is, "If I can't see it, it can't hurt me."

P

pain tolerance—Your ability to physically and psychologically withstand pain.

panic—The second stage of fear; overpowering fear. See fright and terror.

parry—A defensive technique: a quick, forceful slap that redirects an assailant's linear attack. There are two types of parries: horizontal and vertical.

passive response—One of the three possible counters when assaulted by a grab, choke, or hold from a standing position. Passive response requires you to nullify the assault without injuring your adversary. See aggressive response and moderate response.

patience—A combative attribute. The ability to endure and tolerate difficulty.

perception—Interpretation of vital information acquired from your senses when faced with a potentially threatening situation.

philosophical resolution—The act of analyzing and answering various questions concerning the use of violence in defense of yourself and others.

philosophy—One of the five aspects of CFA's mental component. A deep state of introspection whereby you methodically resolve critical questions concerning the use of force in defense of yourself or others.

physical attributes—The numerous physical qualities that enhance your combative skills and abilities.

physical component—One of the three vital components of the CFA system. The physical component includes the physical aspects of fighting, such as physical fitness, weapon/technique mastery, and combative attributes. See mental component and spiritual component.

physical conditioning—See combative fitness.

physical fitness—See combative fitness.

positional asphyxia—The arrangement, placement, or positioning of your opponent's body in such a way as to interrupt your breathing and cause unconsciousness or possibly death.

positioning—The spatial relationship of the assailant to the assailed person in terms of target exposure, escape, angle of attack, and various other strategic considerations.

postal attack - see going postal.

power—A physical attribute of armed and unarmed combat. The amount of force you can generate when striking an anatomical target.

power generators—Specific points on your body that generate impact power. There are three anatomical power generators: shoulders, hips, and feet.

precision—See accuracy.

preemptive strike—See first strike.

premise—An axiom, concept, rule, or any other valid reason to modify or go beyond that which has been established.

preparedness—A state of being ready for combat. There are three components of preparedness: affective preparedness, cognitive preparedness, and psychomotor preparedness.

probable reaction dynamics - The opponent's anticipated or predicted movements or actions during both armed and unarmed combat.

proficiency training—A CFA training methodology requiring the practitioner to execute a specific body weapon, technique, maneuver, or tactic over and over for a prescribed number of repetitions. See conditioning training and street training.

progressive indirect attack (PIA) – One of the five methods of attack. A progressive method of attack whereby the initial tool or technique is designed to set the opponent up for follow-up blows.

proxemics—The study of the nature and effect of man's personal space.

The 10 Best Ways to Defeat Multiple Attackers

proximity—The ability to maintain a strategically safe distance from a threatening individual.

pseudospeciation—A combative attribute. The tendency to assign subhuman and inferior qualities to a threatening assailant.

psychological conditioning—The process of conditioning the mind for the horrors and rigors of real combat.

psychomotor preparedness—One of the three components of preparedness. Psychomotor preparedness means possessing all of the physical skills and attributes necessary to defeat a formidable adversary. See affective preparedness and cognitive preparedness.

punch—A quick, forceful strike of the fists.

punching range—One of the three ranges of unarmed combat. Punching range is the mid range of unarmed combat from which the fighter uses his hands to strike his assailant. See kicking range and grappling range.

punching-range tools—The various body weapons that are employed in the punching range of unarmed combat, including finger jabs, palm-heel strikes, rear cross, knife-hand strikes, horizontal and shovel hooks, uppercuts, and hammer-fist strikes. See grappling-range tools and kicking-range tools.

Q

qualities of combat—See attributes of combat.

quarter beat - One of the four beat classifications of the Widow Maker Program. Quarter beat strikes never break contact with the assailant's face. Quarter beat strikes are primarily responsible for creating the psychological panic and trauma when Razing.

R

range—The spatial relationship between a fighter and a threatening assailant.

range deficiency—The inability to effectively fight and defend in all ranges of combat (armed and unarmed).

range manipulation—A combative attribute. The strategic manipulation of combat ranges.

range proficiency—A combative attribute. The ability to effectively fight and defend in all ranges of combat (armed and unarmed).

ranges of engagement—See combat ranges.

ranges of unarmed combat—The three distances (kicking range, punching range, and grappling range) a fighter might physically engage with an assailant while involved in unarmed combat.

raze – To level, demolish or obliterate.

razer – One who performs the Razing methodology.

razing – The second phase of the Widow Maker Program. A series of vicious close quarter techniques designed to physically and psychologically extirpate a criminal attacker.

razing amplifier - a technique, tactic or procedure that magnifies the destructiveness of your razing technique.

reaction dynamics—see probable reaction dynamics.

reaction time—The elapsed time between a stimulus and the response to that particular stimulus. See offensive reaction time and defensive reaction time.

rear cross—A straight punch delivered from the rear hand that crosses from right to left (if in a left stance) or left to right (if in a right stance).

rear side—The side of the body furthest from the assailant. See lead side.

reasonable force—That degree of force which is not excessive for a particular event and which is appropriate in protecting yourself or others.

refinement—The strategic and methodical process of improving or perfecting.

relocation principle—Also known as relocating, this is a street-fighting tactic that requires you to immediately move to a new location (usually by flanking your adversary) after delivering a compound attack.

repetition—Performing a single movement, exercise, strike, or action continuously for a specific period.

research—A scientific investigation or inquiry.

rhythm—Movements characterized by the natural ebb and flow of related elements.

ritual-oriented training—Formalized training that is conducted without intrinsic purpose. See combat-oriented training and sport-oriented training.

S

safety—One of the three criteria for a CFA body weapon, technique, maneuver, or tactic. It means that the tool, technique, maneuver or tactic provides the least amount of danger and risk for the practitioner. See efficiency and effectiveness.

scissors hold—See guard position.

scorching – Quickly and inconspicuously applying oleoresin capsicum (hot pepper extract) on your fingertips and then razing your adversary.

self-awareness—One of the three categories of CFA awareness. Knowing and understanding yourself. This includes aspects of yourself which may provoke criminal violence and which will promote a proper and strong reaction to an attack. See criminal awareness and situational awareness.

self-confidence—Having trust and faith in yourself.

self-enlightenment—The state of knowing your capabilities, limitations, character traits, feelings, general attributes, and motivations. See self-awareness.

set—A term used to describe a grouping of repetitions.

shadow fighting—A CFA training exercise used to develop and refine your tools, techniques, and attributes of armed and unarmed combat.

sharking – A counter attack technique that is used when your adversary grabs your razing hand.

shielding wedge - a defensive maneuver used to counter an unarmed postal attack.

simple direct attack (SDA) – One of the five methods of attack. A method of attack whereby the practitioner delivers a solitary offenses tool or technique. It may involve a series of discrete probes or one swift, powerful strike aimed at terminating the encounter.

situational awareness—One of the three categories of CFA awareness. A state of being totally alert to your immediate surroundings, including people, places, objects, and actions. (See criminal awareness and self-awareness.)

skeletal alignment—The proper alignment or arrangement of your body. Skeletal alignment maximizes the structural integrity of striking tools.

skills—One of the three factors that determine who will win a street fight. Skills refers to psychomotor proficiency with the tools and techniques of combat. See Attitude and Knowledge.

slipping—A defensive maneuver that permits you to avoid an assailant's linear blow without stepping out of range. Slipping can be accomplished by quickly snapping the head and upper torso sideways (right or left) to avoid the blow.

snap back—A defensive maneuver that permits you to avoid an assailant's linear and circular blows without stepping out of range. The snap back can be accomplished by quickly snapping the head backward to avoid the assailant's blow.

somatotypes—A method of classifying human body types or builds into three different categories: endomorph, mesomorph, and ectomorph. See endomorph, mesomorph, and ectomorph.

sparring—A training exercise where two or more fighters fight each other while wearing protective equipment.

speed—A physical attribute of armed and unarmed combat. The rate or a measure of the rapid rate of motion.

spiritual component—One of the three vital components of the CFA system. The spiritual component includes the metaphysical issues and aspects of existence. See physical component and mental component.

sport-oriented training—Training that is geared for competition and governed by a set of rules. See combat-oriented training and ritual-oriented training.

sprawling—A grappling technique used to counter a double- or single-leg takedown.

square off—To be face-to-face with a hostile or threatening assailant who is about to attack you.

stance—One of the many strategic postures you assume prior to or during armed or unarmed combat.

stick fighting—Fighting that takes place with either one or two sticks.

strategic positioning—Tactically positioning yourself to either escape, move behind a barrier, or use a makeshift weapon.

strategic/tactical development—One of the five elements of CFA's mental component.

strategy—A carefully planned method of achieving your goal of engaging an assailant under advantageous conditions.

street fight—A spontaneous and violent confrontation between two or more individuals wherein no rules apply.

street fighter   An unorthodox combatant who has no formal training. His combative skills and tactics are usually developed in the street by the process of trial and error.

street training—A CFA training methodology requiring the practitioner to deliver explosive compound attacks for 10 to 20 seconds. See condition ng training and proficiency training.

strength training—The process of developing muscular strength through systematic application of progressive resistance.

striking art—A combat art that relies predominantly on striking techniques to neutralize or terminate a criminal attacker.

striking shield—A rectangular shield constructed of foam and vinyl used to develop power in your kicks, punches, and strikes.

striking tool—A natural body weapon that impacts with the assailant's anatomical target.

strong side—The strongest and most coordinated side of your body.

structure—A definite and organized pattern.

style—The distinct manner in which a fighter executes or performs his combat skills.

stylistic integration—The purposeful and scientific collection of tools and techniques from various disciplines, which are strategically integrated and dramatically altered to meet three essential criteria: efficiency, effectiveness, and combative safety.

submission holds—Also known as control and restraint techniques, many of these locks and holds create sufficient pain to cause the adversary to submit.

system—The unification of principles, philosophies, rules, strategies, methodologies, tools, and techniques of a particular method of combat.

T

tactic—The skill of using the available means to achieve an end.

target awareness—A combative attribute that encompasses five strategic principles: target orientation, target recognition, target selection, target impaction, and target exploitation.

target exploitation—A combative attribute. The strategic maximization of your assailant's reaction dynamics during a fight. Target exploitation can be applied in both armed and unarmed encounters.

target impaction—The successful striking of the appropriate anatomical target.

target orientation—A combative attribute. Having a workable knowledge of the assailant's anatomical targets.

target recognition—The ability to immediately recognize appropriate anatomical targets during an emergency self-defense situation.

target selection—The process of mentally selecting the appropriate anatomical target for your self-defense situation. This is predicated on certain factors, including proper force response, assailant's positioning, and range.

target stare—A form of telegraphing in which you stare at the anatomical target you intend to strike.

target zones—The three areas in which an assailant's anatomical targets are located. (See zone one, zone two and zone three.)

technique—A systematic procedure by which a task is accomplished.

telegraphic cognizance—A combative attribute. The ability to recognize both verbal and non-verbal signs of aggression or assault.

telegraphing—Unintentionally making your intentions known to your adversary.

tempo—The speed or rate at which you speak.

terminate—To kill.

terror—The third stage of fear; defined as overpowering fear. See fright and panic.

timing—A physical and mental attribute of armed and unarmed combat. Your ability to execute a movement at the optimum moment.

tone—The overall quality or character of your voice.

tool—See body weapon.

traditional martial arts—Any martial art that fails to evolve and change to meet the demands and characteristics of its present environment.

traditional style/system—See traditional martial arts.

training drills—The various exercises and drills aimed at perfecting combat skills, attributes, and tactics.

trap and tuck – A counter move technique used when the adversary attempts to raze you during your quarter beat assault.

U

unified mind—A mind free and clear of distractions and focused on the combative situation.

use of force response—A combative attribute. Selecting the appropriate level of force for a particular emergency self-defense situation.

V

viciousness—A combative attribute. The propensity to be extremely violent and destructive often characterized by intense savagery.

violence—The intentional utilization of physical force to coerce, injure, cripple, or kill.

visualization—Also known as mental visualization or mental imagery. The purposeful formation of mental images and scenarios in the mind's eye.

W

warm-up—A series of mild exercises, stretches, and movements designed to prepare you for more intense exercise.

weak side—The weaker and more uncoordinated side of your body.

weapon and technique mastery—A component of CFA's physical component. The kinesthetic and psychomotor development of a weapon or combative technique.

weapon capability—An assailant's ability to use and attack with a particular weapon.

webbing - The first phase of the Widow Maker Program. Webbing is a two hand strike delivered to the assailant's chin. It is called Webbing because your hands resemble a large web that wraps around the enemy's face.

widow maker – One who makes widows by destroying husbands.

widow maker program – A CFA combat program specifically designed to teach the law abiding citizen how to use extreme force when faced with immediate threat of unlawful deadly criminal attack. The Widow Maker program is divided into two phases or methodologies: Webbing and Razing.

Y

yell—A loud and aggressive scream or shout used for various strategic reasons.

Z

zero beat – One of the four beat classifications of the Widow Maker, Feral Fighting and Savage Street Fighting Programs. Zero beat strikes are full pressure techniques applied to a specific target until it completely ruptures. They include gouging, crushing, biting, and choking techniques.

zone one—Anatomical targets related to your senses, including the eyes, temple, nose, chin, and back of neck.

zone three—Anatomical targets related to your mobility, including thighs, knees, shins, and instep.

zone two—Anatomical targets related to your breathing, including front of neck, solar plexus, ribs, and groin.

The 10 Best Ways to Defeat Multiple Attackers

About Sammy Franco

With over 30 years of experience, Sammy Franco is one of the world's foremost authorities on armed and unarmed self-defense. Highly regarded as a leading innovator in combat sciences, Mr. Franco was one of the premier pioneers in the field of "reality-based" self-defense and martial arts instruction.

Sammy Franco is perhaps best known as the founder and creator of Contemporary Fighting Arts (CFA), a state-of-the-art offensive-based combat system that is specifically designed for real-world self-defense. CFA is a sophisticated and practical system of self-defense, designed specifically to provide efficient and effective methods to avoid, defuse, confront, and neutralize both armed and unarmed attackers.

Sammy Franco has frequently been featured in martial art magazines, newspapers, and appeared on numerous radio and television programs. Mr. Franco has also authored numerous books, magazine articles, and editorials, and has developed a popular library of instructional videos.

Sammy Franco's experience and credibility in the combat sciences is unequaled. One of his many accomplishments in this field includes the fact that he has earned the ranking of a Law Enforcement Master Instructor, and has designed, implemented, and taught officer survival training to the United States Border Patrol (USBP). He has instructed members of the US Secret Service, Military Special Forces,

The 10 Best Ways to Defeat Multiple Attackers

Washington DC Police Department, Montgomery County, Maryland Deputy Sheriffs, and the US Library of Congress Police. Sammy Franco is also a member of the prestigious International Law Enforcement Educators and Trainers Association (ILEETA) as well as the American Society of Law Enforcement Trainers (ASLET) and he is listed in the "Who's Who Director of Law Enforcement Instructors."

Sammy Franco is a nationally certified Law Enforcement Instructor in the following curricula: PR-24 Side-Handle Baton, Police Arrest and Control Procedures, Police Personal Weapons Tactics, Police Power Handcuffing Methods, Police Oleoresin Capsicum Aerosol Training (OCAT), Police Weapon Retention and Disarming Methods, Police Edged Weapon Countermeasures and "Use of Force" Assessment and Response Methods.

Mr. Franco holds a Bachelor of Arts degree in Criminal Justice from the University of Maryland. He is a regularly featured speaker at a number of professional conferences and conducts dynamic and enlightening seminars on numerous aspects of self-defense and combat training.

On a personal level, Sammy Franco is an animal lover, who will go to great lengths to assist and rescue animals. Throughout the years, he's rescued everything from turkey vultures to goats. However, his most treasured moments are always spent with his beloved German Shepherd dogs.

For more information about Mr. Franco and his unique Contemporary Fighting Arts system, you can visit his website at: **SammyFranco.com** or follow him on twitter **@RealSammyFranco**

Other Books by Sammy Franco

KILLER INSTINCT
Unarmed Combat for Street Survival
by Sammy Franco

Here, Mr. Franco describes the mental, spiritual and physical components of his advanced system of combat that offers the fighter a brutal and efficient arsenal. But a weapon is only as good as the soldier trained to use it. Reading this book is the first step. Followed by proper and consistent training, the tools and techniques contained herein can be maximized by the martial artists who has attained self-knowledge, psychological preparedness and most importantly, mastery of the killer instinct. 8.5 x 5.5, paperback, photos, illus, 134 pages.

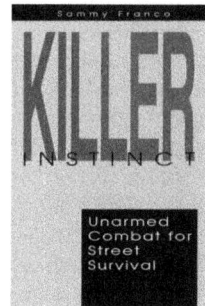

INVINCIBLE
Mental Toughness Techniques for Peak Performance
by Sammy Franco

Invincible is a treasure trove of battle-tested techniques and strategies for improving mental toughness in all aspects of life. It teaches you how to unlock the true power of your mind and achieve success in sports, fitness, high-risk professions, self-defense, and other peak performance activities. However, you don't have to be an athlete or warrior to benefit from this unique mental toughness book. In fact, the mental skills featured in this indispensable program can be used by anyone who wants to reach their full potential in life. 8.5 x 5.5, paperback, photos, illus, 250 pages.

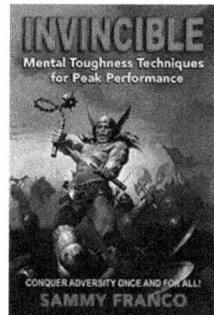

WARRIOR WISDOM
Inspiring Ideas from the World's Greatest Warriors
by Sammy Franco

Warrior Wisdom includes a huge collection of unforgettable quotes, sayings and writings from warriors and warrior leaders, both past and present, and from around the world. This exhaustive book reveals the essentialities of the Fighter's life, speaking with great heart, eloquence, wisdom and an earned authenticity on subjects still crucial to you today: leadership, loyalty, honor, courage, tactics, strategy and much more. Warrior Wisdom offers a unique opportunity to thoroughly explore what it really means to be a warrior...in the worlds of yesterday and today! 7 x 10, paperback, 216 pages.

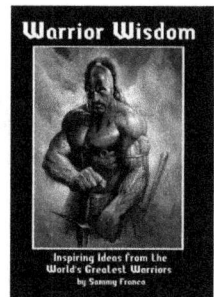

SAVAGE STREET FIGHTING
Tactical Savagery as a Last Resort
by Sammy Franco

In this revolutionary book, Sammy Franco reveals the science behind his most primal street fighting method. Savage Street Fighting is a brutal self-defense system specifically designed to teach the law-abiding citizen how to use "Tactical Savagery" when faced with the immediate threat of an unlawful deadly criminal attack. Savage Street Fighting is systematically engineered to protect you when there are no other self-defense options left! With over 300 photographs and detailed step-by-step instructions, Savage Street Fighting is a must-have book for anyone concerned about real world self-defense. Now is the time to learn how to unleash your inner beast! 8.5 x 5.5, paperback, 317 photos, illustrations, 232 pages.

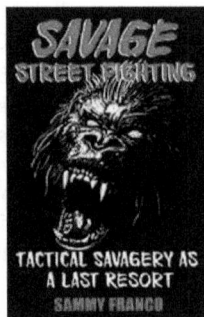

FIRST STRIKE
End a Fight in Ten Seconds or Less!
by Sammy Franco

Learn how to stop any attack before it starts by mastering the art of the preemptive strike. First Strike gives you an easy-to-learn yet highly effective self-defense game plan for handling violent close-quarter combat encounters. First Strike will teach you instinctive, practical and realistic self-defense techniques that will drop any criminal attacker to the floor with one punishing blow. By reading this book and by practicing, you will learn the hard-hitting skills necessary to execute a punishing first strike and ultimately prevail in a self-defense situation. And that's what it is all about: winning in as little time as possible. 8.5 x 5.5, paperback, photos, illustrations, 202 pages.

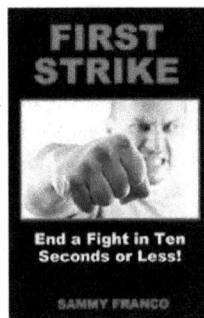

WAR MACHINE
How to Transform Yourself Into A Vicious & Deadly Street Fighter
by Sammy Franco

War Machine is a book that will change you for the rest of your life! When followed accordingly, War Machine will forge your mind, body and spirit into iron. Once armed with the mental and physical attributes of the War Machine, you will become a strong and confident warrior that can handle just about anything that life may throw your way. In essence, War Machine is a way of life. Powerful, intense, and hard. 11 x 8.5, paperback, photos, illustrations, 210 pages.

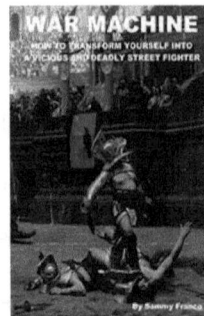

124

KUBOTAN POWER
Quick and Simple Steps to Mastering the Kubotan Keychain
by Sammy Franco

With over 290 photographs and step-by-step instructions, Kubotan Power is the authoritative resource for mastering this devastating self-defense weapon. In this one-of-a-kind book, world-renowned self-defense expert, Sammy Franco takes thirty years of real-world teaching experience and gives you quick, easy and practical kubotan techniques that can be used by civilians, law enforcement personnel, or military professionals. The Kubotan is an incredible self-defense weapon that has helped thousands of people effectively defend themselves. Men, women, law enforcement officers, military, and security professionals alike, appreciate this small and discreet self-defense tool. Unfortunately, however, very little has been written about the kubotan, leaving it shrouded in both mystery and ignorance. As a result, most people don't know how to unleash the full power of this unique personal defense weapon. 8.5 x 5.5, paperback, 290 photos, illustrations, 204 pages.

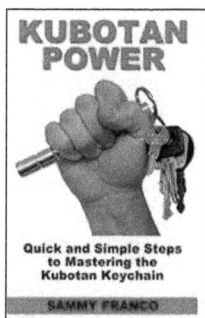

THE COMPLETE BODY OPPONENT BAG BOOK
by Sammy Franco

In this one-of-a-kind book, Sammy Franco teaches you the many hidden training features of the body opponent bag that will improve your fighting skills and boost your conditioning. With detailed photographs, step-by-step instructions, and dozens of unique workout routines, The Complete Body Opponent Bag Book is the authoritative resource for mastering this lifelike punching bag. The Complete Body Opponent Bag Book covers stances, punching, kicking, grappling techniques, mobility and footwork, targets, fighting ranges, training gear, time based workouts, punching and kicking combinations, weapons training, grappling drills, ground fighting, and dozens of workouts that will challenge you for years to come. 8.5 x 5.5, paperback, 139 photos, illustrations, 206 pages.

125